HAUNTED SCHOOLS OF ARIZONA

DEBE BRANNING

Haunted America

Published by Haunted America
A Division of The History Press
Charleston, SC
www.historypress.com

Front cover image courtesy of Chance Houston; back cover inset image courtesy of the author; back cover bottom image courtesy of Tamara Geiger McGinnitty.

First published 2024

Manufactured in the United States

ISBN 9781467156295

Library of Congress Control Number: 2024936748

To all the wonderful teachers at Corrigan Elementary School and William Jennings Bryan Junior/Senior High School in Omaha, Nebraska, who always let me express my wild and creative imagination in my writing.

CONTENTS

ACKNOWLEDGEMENTS

I would like to give a big thank-you to all the knowledgeable paranormal investigative teams, tour guides, tour companies, historians and amazing location owners who willingly shared their information, experiences and tales of the unknown to fill these pages with the phenomena they encountered. I also want to thank the friends and team members who have accompanied me while I've explored various schools and locations throughout the years and participated in the interviews. A special thanks goes to the friends who helped photograph some of these historic schools and Vanna, who helped with editing.

As I continue to say, history and mystery go hand in hand. And I am hoping these stories will carry on the school spirit of these houses of education for many years to come.

INTRODUCTION

Old schools and universities are bound to have histories with a few tragic events that could attract the spirits of former students or faculty members. School buildings may have hauntings due to the large amount of energy emitted by the students who have studied within its walls. The buildings and playing fields could have absorbed a lot of psychic energy.

Schools have unexplained sounds as creepy as fingernails running across a chalkboard, the warning ring of the tardy bell and the annoying squeak of an old dried-up Magic Marker.

Some schools claim to be built on ancient burial grounds or constructed over forgotten cemeteries. Other buildings were erected on the sites of tragic suicides, murders or unexplained deaths.

There are schools that shrug off tales of having an alleged haunted history, while other learning facilities embrace their reputation for all things paranormal. I guess it depends on the "principal" of the matter.

So, why are schools haunted? Dedicated teachers, principals and classroom aides who loved their professions continue to watch over their old classrooms. Janitors remain at the school buildings and continue to stoke the heat from archaic boiler rooms, correct flickering lighting fixtures by climbing tall ladders and sweep floors with wide push brooms and mops.

The grade school I attended, Corrigan School in Omaha, Nebraska, was built in 1900. There were staircases that had no handrails that led to the upper floors and down to the basement level. There was no air conditioning during the humid months, and students used cloakrooms—open hallways adjacent to the classroom—to hang their jackets and sweaters and store their umbrellas and wet boots. My school was demolished in 1984, and boy, I really wanted a "brick in the wall."

My junior/senior high school was considerably more modern, having been constructed in 1964 and 1965. It was the typical two-level building of the day, spread out in the suburbs with an adjoining cafeteria and gymnasium. We were fortunate to boast an indoor swimming pool, baseball diamond and practice football field. A recent class reunion tour of the building brought back fond memories of being a pompom girl and performing dance routines on the gymnasium floor and having a minor acting part in the musicals on the auditorium stage.

But wait! Whenever I dream at night about being at school, it is always centered on my grade school. I remember the high pressed ceiling tiles, wide hallways and chalkboards that framed the area that made up the large classrooms. It always seems so real! Am I *really* dreaming, or am I subconsciously *haunting* the grounds were the schoolhouse once stood proudly?

And remember, long ago, children felt it was a privilege to go to school—they were not forced to stay back at their home. While attending school, they did not have to do the chores on the farm, clean and cook for the household or tend to their younger siblings. School was their escape from reality. It was a way to move all those grown-up responsibilities to another corner of one's mind. After all, there would be plenty of time for "adulting." It was a time to have fun with lifelong friends. Perhaps that is why I am still in contact with many of my grade school (and junior/senior high) friends!

Disclaimer: Please respect the schools cited in this book. Some of them are working halls of education, while others are historic structures that have been repurposed as museums, hotels and government offices. While many of the ghostly tales are true and backed by researched documents, some of these stories have been handed down through the years and could simply be legend and folklore. Some of the tales come from the views and perspectives of enthusiastic school students and staff. Be true to your school!

1

COCHISE COUNTY

THE SCHOOL HOUSE INN
818 TOMBSTONE CANYON
BISBEE, AZ 85603

The School House Inn started out as Bisbee's Garfield Elementary School and was constructed in 1918. It sits on a hill that overlooks Tombstone Canyon Road. Garfield School was built during Bisbee's growing spree, and it was anticipated that the metropolis of Bisbee was going to expand even more. Then along came World War I and the 1918 influenza pandemic, which brought expansion to a screeching halt. The town's population stabilized, construction in Bisbee began to slow down and additional schools were suddenly not needed.

But for two decades, first through fourth grade students who lived in the homes near the top of Tombstone Canyon received their education in the modern, two-story red brick building. The school closed in 1938 and was refashioned into a much-needed apartment building. Bathrooms were added, and the large classrooms were divided into smaller apartments. Years later, the building was used as a residence for the elderly. It was finally converted into a bed-and-breakfast in the late 1980s, giving tourists a quiet destination within walking distance to the shops, restaurants and saloons that Bisbee has to offer.

School House Inn at the top of Tombstone Canyon. *Author's collection.*

The School House Inn maintains its original theme as a place of learning. Each of its nine guest rooms has a school-themed name. Guests can choose from former classrooms, including the Art Room, Geography Room, Music Room, History Room and Reading Room, and a larger group is welcomed to spend time in the Principal's Office Suite.

The owners from the early 2000s, John Lambert and Paula Roth, graciously took care of everything at the inn, including making breakfast, cleaning rooms, manicuring the grounds and offering history lessons of the area to the guests. They enjoyed educating visitors on some of the recurring ghost tales.

The MVD Ghostchasers hosted a Paranormal PJ Party investigation at the School House Inn in February 2014. The sold-out event brought in twenty-eight paranormal investigators who belonged to seven paranormal teams located throughout Arizona and Nevada to Bisbee.

The much-anticipated event began at 3:00 p.m. with check-in and a meet-and-greet social hour that included soft drinks and snacks. A paranormal swap meet table was set up for folks to sell or trade various pieces of ghost hunting equipment. Pizza was delivered, and while everyone enjoyed a much-needed dinner hour, innkeeper John told the group about some of the haunting experiences that have mystified the guests in the various classrooms.

The innkeepers had placed various antique toys in the hallways as part of the décor. Paula Roth liked to talk about the time she walked past the antique doll carriage positioned along the wall in the hallway. She was preparing the rooms for the evening guests, carrying towels and linen, dashing up and down the hall. She had to take a second look when she almost tripped over the doll carriage that somehow ended up in the middle of the hallway. The paranormal investigators did various tests to check the evenness and vibrations of the floor and found nothing that would have caused the object to move on its own.

Other guests have seen shadows walk past their room doors and noted an apparition of a woman walking around in their guest room. Are they teachers? Guests? Residents of the former home for the elderly? We may never know.

Guest speaker Francine Powers gave a powerful account of growing up in the most haunted house in the city of Bisbee, which just happened to be located on a property directly behind the School House Inn. One could hardly imagine the horrors her parents and siblings witnessed in the home where a very rare order of exorcism was performed by the Tucson Catholic Diocese. There was a hush in the air as the group followed Francine to the roadway that faces the menacing house. Francine told a few more stories about the historic home and advised the groups to return later in smaller teams to do further investigations, as long as they remained on the roadway and kept off the private property.

Everyone dashed to their rooms to change into their official School House Inn T-shirts to pose for a "class picture" on the inn's staircase. The group looked like a madcap party on a twisty roller-coaster ride! Some teams walked the hallways of the inn and discovered the presence of some of the former dedicated teaching staff. Midnight found the paranormal groups visiting the site of the "scary house" in the hopes of making contact with the spirits within.

Conversations and theories were discussed into the wee hours of the night, but everyone was up bright and early, just in time for a full cooked breakfast served by innkeepers John and Paula. Everyone agreed the School House Inn was the perfect retreat for seasoned ghost hunters to discover lessons learned and explore the mining town ghosts.

LOWELL MIDDLE SCHOOL
100 OLD DOUGLAS ROAD
BISBEE, AZ 85603

Lowell was, at one time, a sizable mining town located just to the southeast of the metropolis of Old Bisbee. The majority of the original town's site was swallowed by the excavation of the Lavender Pit Mine during the 1950s. All that remains today is a small portion of Erie Street, along with Evergreen Cemetery, the Saginaw subdivision and Lowell Middle School. Lowell is now considered more of a place name than an actual community.

The 1931 Lowell School was constructed near Highway 81 along Old Douglas Road, a once busy highway that carried traffic between Bisbee and Douglas. The school was built for the children who lived in the nearby mining towns of Lowell, South Bisbee, the Johnson Addition and Tin Town. At one time, over seven hundred boys and girls were enrolled at the two-story brick school.

The cornerstone ceremony was held at the school on February 15, 1931, conducted by the Masonic Grand Lodge of Arizona.

A gymnasium and cafeteria were added in 1976. Lowell School was considered one of the finest schools in southern Arizona. The tradition of the school serving the needs of the Bisbee community continues, and the one-thousand-seat auditorium has been the scene of many concerts, plays and events.

Visitors marvel at the majestic doorway at the front entrance of the school. It is graced with a set of double doors made of solid copper. The two doors weigh a total of eight hundred pounds and remain proud reminders of Bisbee's copper mining district. The roof of the school is said to be constructed of another sixteen tons of copper.

The neighboring area holds many underground copper mines, crystal caves and an occasional flow of water in the wash just west of the Lowell School. Along with the beautiful, historic Evergreen Cemetery directly across the road, these elements can easily be explained as possible conduits for the haunting of the historic school.

Author Francine Powers (*Haunted Bisbee*, 2020) grew up in Bisbee and attended Lowell Middle School from sixth grade through eighth grade. She noted that a classroom situated near the location of the old janitor's apartment seemed to harbor the most paranormal activity. Lights in the

Historic Lowell Middle School. *Author's collection.*

room often flickered on and off, and books slammed shut and often made the hair on your arms stand on end!

Having a school across from a cemetery can have a positive effect, too. Francine also noted that members of the sports teams and students who arrive from out of town for away games have seen strange lights floating over grave markers in the historic graveyard, perhaps a welcoming sign for the evening's victory!

TWO CROWS HAUNTED FRANKLIN PUBLIC SCHOOL
DOUGLAS, AZ 85607

They say when crows appear on the scene, it is a signal that change is coming in the world. If they are always around you, there could be a change centered on you or your lifestyle.

Crows appeared at Franklin School in Douglas. *Wikimedia.*

In September 1909, it was stated that for many years, two crows flew into a Douglas, Arizona neighborhood to roost on the old Franklin Public School's turrets. The elementary school, no longer standing, sat on the southeast corner of Thirteenth Avenue and H Street near the downtown area of Douglas. The strange mystery is that the birds were seen at the school only on Saturdays, Sundays and holidays. The presence and noise of the schoolchildren on the school's grounds might have been what kept the crows away. The crows were never seen during school hours, only on holidays, when there was no school scheduled and no children present.

Saturdays and Sundays may (by some sort of count of time in the nature of the crows) be known to them. *But what about the occasional holiday?* Holidays are irregular, but the crows seemed to know when one popped up on the calendar. Without a doubt, you could find them sitting on the school turrets all day. Those who observed the birds knew where they roosted. Sometimes, they flew in one direction, and other days, they soared in the opposite direction.

There were also two colonies of crows around the nation's capital, Washington, D.C. One lived out in Columbia Heights on the northern end of the city, and the other lived on the Virginia shore at the base of the hills of Arlington. It was said by people who studied "crowology" that neither flock ever crossed the Potomac River.

There was another old crow that paid a weekly visit to the equestrian statue of Brevet Lieutenant General Winfield Scott. It usually circled the head of the general, flopped down for a minute and then flew away, cawing as it flew. The visit was not made on any particular day, but people in the area noticed it occurred about once every seven days.

There is only an empty lot where Franklin School once stood. You can still drive to the spot and watch for the crows on the weekends and holidays. From Phoenix, it is about a 233-mile drive—or 202 miles as the crow flies.

GLEESON SCHOOL
GLEESON, AZ 85610

Gleeson (originally the Turquoise town site) was the location of early turquoise deposits mined by the local Natives. The decorative stones became a vital part of early trade in the area. The village was renamed in honor of John Gleeson, a prospector from the nearby town of Pearce. It thrived on copper taken from the Shannon Mine from about 1909 to World War I. As the population of Gleeson began to grow, so did the need for education and schools.

As it was in all early Arizona mining towns, education was an important factor for families with children in Gleeson. Gleeson's first schoolhouse was merely a small building established in the downtown business district. Gleeson's population continued to flourish, and soon, there was a need for a second school. This second schoolhouse was built of wood and sat across the road from the notorious Gleeson Jail.

Gleeson (now a popular city along the Ghost Town Trail) soon boasted a hospital, homes, a theater, general stores and a dozen restaurants and bars. The town had a large Mexican population because Mexican miners were allowed to work in the underground mines (for which the wages were higher). In Bisbee, Mexicans could work only the lower-paying positions on the surface level.

Construction of the third and final school lasted from late 1917 through 1918 at a cost of $65,000. The classroom teachers were ready for students in the 1918–19 school year. The new school was constructed of sturdy concrete. It had one floor for classrooms and a basement designed to hold storage items. When the Arizona weather became uninviting, the children would hold recess in the cooler basement. Gleeson School was set up to cover first through eighth grades. High school students traveled the extra miles over to Tombstone for their studies. Some students lived with family members who resided in Bisbee or Douglas to attend high school and returned to Gleeson only on holidays or school breaks.

From 1900 to the mid-1920s, Gleeson's population grew steadily and the teachers at the school were able to educate over one thousand students. However, by 1929, Gleeson's mining output had begun to decline, and the people who worked in and depended on the mines left. Gleeson eventually lost its post office in 1939.

Between the two world wars, the price of copper fell, and with it fell the fortunes of Gleeson. By 1930, the town's hospital was in disrepair, and the

Gleeson School ruins. *Courtesy of Tamara Geiger McGinnitty.*

number of local businesses had shrunk to only a handful. Ranching had become the primary means of making a living in the area, and by 1938, the Gleeson School had closed for good. The remaining students merged with classes at schools in the Tombstone School District.

After the schoolhouse was closed, the final operations of the mine were about wrapped up in 1940, with a complete shutdown in 1953. Gleeson School was dismantled to provide timbers for the mines and other buildings in the Tombstone area. The strong wooden floorboards were removed and used for new flooring at the Crystal Palace in Tombstone. The amazing archway that showcased the school's entrance has remained standing for a good number of years.

Rhonda and Dwight Hull, who direct paranormal investigations with Beelieve Paranormal, reported some of their haunted experiences that occurred while they explored the deserted ghost town ruins with other interested ghost hunters. Rhonda said,

> *On our last trip to Gleeson, we took a group of investigators out with us and conducted an EVP session. Our Rem Pod was also turned on. We had a visit from the "janitor." He interacted with us and answered various questions under the guidance of the Rem Pod.*

We also encountered the spirit of a young girl who kept tapping one of our guests on the shoulder. The spirited young girl lifted the guest's pink, flowery adorned headband.

During the 2017 A Haunting in the Desert event (a ghost hunting weekend organized by the Hulls), several of the invited guests and distinguished paranormal celebrities caravanned in vehicles to the ghost town of Gleeson for a daytime investigation. The group hiked down the pathway to the remains of the old Gleeson School building. Carefully watching out for springtime rattlesnakes, the group climbed down into the inner sanctum ruins of the shell-like structure. They could feel the presence of curious schoolchildren gathering around the visiting urban explorers.

Debe Branning held up a digital recorder and asked the spirits, "Did you go to school here?" After a pause, the digital recorder responded by picking up a wispy female voice that said, "Yes." Several of the guests heard the spirit's voice audibly.

Gleeson School has been used for weddings, theatrical performances and revival-style evangelistic services. In 1916, one newspaper reported the schoolhouse hosted an exhibition by a man and wife who posed as mediums. They darkened the room and conjured mysterious phenomena to beguile the awestruck crowd. "Hands were seen, a guitar was made to give forth music by invisible hands, writing was in an unexplainable manner, and several other manifestations entertained the audience in a very satisfactory manner."

But not everyone may know that Gleeson is the location for one of the most widespread UFO sightings in Arizona. On August 26, 1968, Pearl Christiansen, a seventy-one-year-old retired Gleeson schoolteacher, was driving up to her ranch house when she noticed a large, silver circular object hovering on the south side of Brown's Peak. "It looked as though there were a train of strange lights trailing from one side. Then I saw a second object— very shiny and gold. They both were stationary and every once in a while, both would glow simultaneously."

"I was happily excited about the beauty of the thing," Pearl was quoted as saying. "I never was afraid. I had no fear—just excited."

Pearl Christiansen described the UFOs as having a red band that turned a wine-like color, then turned purple and then, several minutes later, gold. Up at the ranch house, Pearl grabbed a pair of binoculars and kept watch over the strange object. "The object appeared blurred," she noted, "It also hurt my eyes to look at its brightness."

The objects hovered for hours that night. Then they seemed to back away into the valley beyond Brown's Peak. In the next few days after the sighting, Pearl and her friends ventured to the site of the UFO, where they found burned cactuses, badly burned rocks and an odd acid-like smell. A report was filed with the National Investigations Committee on Aerial Phenomena in December 1968.

A native of the Colorado Territory, Pearl Johnson Christianson moved to Gleeson in 1920 to teach the youngsters of the town's eighty-one mining community families. She later met her husband and became a ranch wife and part-time teacher.

An epic western movie was filmed in Gleeson in 1938. The film was an adaptation of the popular Zane Grey novel *The Mysterious Rider*. In short, the story centers on Ben Wade and his partner Frosty, who return to the Bellounds' ranch, where, twenty years earlier, Wade was wanted for murder. Unrecognized, he gets a job on the ranch and soon becomes involved in Folsom's cattle rustling and a chance to settle an old score.

Revival evangelistic services? Spirit séances? UFOs? Mystery movies? No wonder the Gleeson School spirits are so lively!

TOMBSTONE UNION HIGH SCHOOL
645 EAST FREMONT STREET
TOMBSTONE, AZ 85638

Tombstone Union High School was a large historic high school in Tombstone, Arizona. The two-story structure was the only high school in the Tombstone Unified School District for many years. The school and its main building were opened in 1922 on 605 East Fremont Street, serving students from Fairbanks, Gleeson, Huachuca City and Tombstone. In 1951, a new gym was built; a few years later, modern dressing rooms were added. A new industrial arts building was erected in 1963. In the 1970s, an addition to the gym was constructed; it housed the band room and sports activity room. The year 1983 saw two new science rooms added on the west side of the school. In 1990, a new Ramada locker facility was added on the east side. A new bus garage at the district office was also completed. A new high school cafeteria enhanced the campus, located next to the art room at the district office. It began full operations the first part of

Tombstone Union High School. *Courtesy of Tamara Geiger McGinnitty.*

1999 and has fulfilled a long-time need. With the opening of the cafeteria came the closed campus policy.

August 2006 marked the beginning of a new era with the opening of a brand-new Tombstone High School campus just a few miles outside of town off Highway 80. The grand old Tombstone Union High School was closed for good.

The landmark building of old Tombstone Union High School sits on four and a half acres, near the famous Allen Street and Bird Cage Theatre. It still features twelve-foot-high ceilings, original hardwood floors, eight-foot-tall windows and a stage.

Tombstone Union High School was built on land where a red-light district once flourished. There were prostitution cribs, gamblers and notorious gunfighters who occupied the buildings at the east end of Allen Street. Perhaps some of the Wild West remains in the soil of the schoolyard.

Remarkably, there have not been many paranormal investigations allowed at the historic school building. In fact, Rich Donovan (the leader of the Ghost Patrol) can claim the honor of doing one of the only and most thorough explorations of the building in 2009.

Donovan led his crew of ghost hunters to the building at the request of a former student who had a friend who passed away in the girl's locker room near the showers. He was hoping for confirmation that the girl's deceased friend had found peace in the afterlife.

Camera crew footage showed the Ghost Patrol sitting quietly in the locker room, observing their surroundings. The group's medium was getting ready to speak with the spirit of the former student when, suddenly, a dark, shadowy figured walked in front of the camera and crew. It blocked the LR light for just a few seconds before moving past the group. It was an experience none of them will ever forget.

At the time of this writing, the old Tombstone Union High School sits empty, just waiting for that enterprising investor to come along and turn the former place of learning into a modern hotel or a bed-and-breakfast establishment.

2

COCONINO COUNTY

FLAGSTAFF PUBLIC LIBRARY (SITE OF EMERSON SCHOOL)
300 WEST ASPEN AVENUE
FLAGSTAFF, AZ 86001

In 1985, Flagstaff, Arizona, searched for a perfect location to build a new library. The Flagstaff voters approved a $4 million bond issue to erect a modern facility at the site of the old Emerson School. Architects from the firm Snowden and Hopkins designed the spacious thirty-four-thousand-square-foot building. In May 1987, a grand opening was held at the Flagstaff Public Library, which features cathedral ceilings and four fireplaces. The current public library system serves a combined population of approximately 116,000 adults and youth. The library is also known to have a resident spirit, which is playfully called Emerson the ghost.

Emerson School was completed in 1895 and was considered the finest school in Flagstaff. Matt Riordan spoke at the school's dedication ceremony when the cornerstone was placed and sealed. The sturdy two-story schoolhouse was constructed with a deep cellar beneath it. Emerson School served Flagstaff students from 1896 until it was condemned in 1980. The landmark school and its classrooms were dismissed forever and eventually torn down.

The Flagstaff Public Library is featured on the Flagstaff's Haunted Places walking tour presented by the Flagstaff Visitor Center. The tour guide pamphlet relates a tale in which "a former custodian of Emerson School became distraught and killed his family. He then went to the school house and committed suicide in the building."

Research discovered there was once an Emerson School janitor who was strongly attached to his job. Fortunately, there was never a family massacre or suicide involved. But janitor Hugh McGookin was always on the job, making sure the school was clean, the plants were watered and the coal bin was full and ready to keep the students warm. There was an incident when the Flagstaff Fire Department was called to the basement of Emerson School after a spontaneous combustion was reported in the coal bin. Mr. McGookin noted that the coal bin smelled hot and left another gentleman to watch it. It began to smoke, and the man tried to stop it by throwing water on the coal. An explosion of the coal gas made the job look too big for him, so he sounded the fire alarm. Luckily, the coal bin was fireproof, so if there had been much of a fire, it would have been confined to the bin.

Another time, McGookin climbed up on the roof of Emerson School to saw off the remnant of an old pole that had been damaged when lightning struck and knocked off the top.

Many librarians and patrons claim they have seen the janitor's shadowy figure ascending a long-forgotten staircase to the upper floors of the school building that are no longer there. He seems to vanish just as he reaches the top step. Doors in the library open and close on their own, and strange noises are frequently reported throughout the facility.

Mabel Milligan was a dedicated Emerson Elementary School teacher who graduated from the Las Vegas, New Mexico Seminary in 1892. She taught at the Spanish Mission School in Albuquerque for several years before going to Chicago for her postgraduate courses. Mabel was also a graduate of the State Teachers College of Greeley, Colorado, and specialized in teaching kindergarten classes. She taught school in Florence, Denver, Trinidad and other towns in Colorado. In 1918, Mabel moved to Flagstaff to help take care of her elderly parents and resided in a home across the street from the school. She taught first grade at Emerson Elementary School for the next five years.

Mabel's health suddenly declined in the fall of 1923. The frail, dedicated teacher taught at the school for as long as her failing health would allow her. She then checked into Mercy Hospital, where she sadly died on November 8,

Flagstaff Library, the site of Emerson School. *Courtesy of Carolee Jackson.*

1923, in a diabetic coma. She was buried in the GAR Cemetery in Flagstaff. Could Miss Milligan be one of many spirits who still enforce the golden rule?

The librarians have often blamed the current night janitors for moving books, papers and other items after hours when the building is closed. Of course, the cleaning staff denies the accusations of tomfoolery. Is the ghost of Emerson School the result of a residual haunting? Is a spirit now walking the halls without a pass in the Flagstaff Public Library? Check it out for yourself. This library is overdue for a good investigation.

MORTON HALL AT NORTHERN ARIZONA UNIVERSITY
224 MCMULLEN CIRCLE
FLAGSTAFF, AZ 86011

Morton Hall (also referred as North Morton Hall), built in 1914, is one of the oldest buildings on the Northern Arizona University (NAU) campus. It first operated as a woman's dormitory in 1918. The hall was named after

Mary Morton Pollock, who headed the English department and financial assistance office at the school. The three-story Georgian Revival–style structure has been modified several times over the years, but its legendary ghost tale remains the same!

Rumors state the campus is haunted because it was constructed over an "old Indian burial ground." Yet other students and alumni believe its haunt stems from the fact that it is surrounded by three different historic cemeteries.

The ghostly legends surfaced several years ago and have made Morton Hall one of the top haunts of all the NAU campus dorms. The ghost that appears in the all-female residence for upperclassmen is said to be the spirit of a former student who hanged herself in her room during a cold, lonely winter break. Some say the coed fell in love with a soldier who went off to war during World War II and sadly suffered an untimely death in battle. She learned of his demise shortly before Christmas break and was devastated. After the students and staff left for the holidays, the depressed coed remained behind and ended her life.

Another version of the tale has Christmas 1953 as the time stamp. The forlorn nineteen-year-old student was said to have been abandoned by her boyfriend on campus, and to make matters worse, her parents were unable to afford transportation to get the coed home for the holidays. The story states the lonely girl hanged herself with a rope in room 200A, only to be discovered hanging from a bar in the closet by a cleaning crew several days later. An additional rumor states that, after the girl's body was found, a baby was discovered in the basement of the building.

The residents of Morton Hall have given the forlorn spirit the name Kathy, and she has become somewhat of a prankster spirit! She has a habit of locking girls in the bathroom and pulling blankets off the beds while students are sleeping. On rare occasions, her apparition has been seen walking down the hallways. Lights turn on and off, residents hear disturbing scratching sounds on the walls and strange fragrances are noted in the dorm building.

One NAU student reported,

I lived in North Morton for a year. I had a single room on the third floor. This is a pretty active place. The stereos in nearby rooms would kick off full blast when no one was there. My room was next to a closet, and things could be heard moving around at all hours, although the room was completely empty. And then there were noises in my own room. Both myself and various friends experienced the dragging and moving sounds in my

Morton Hall at Northern Arizona University. *Author's collection.*

room. I was never really scared, although the basement could make anyone uneasy. Once, a friend pushed me up all the basement stairs, straight out of a nearby door, insisting someone began pushing her from behind in the basement. The look on her face was all your needed to see to know that she was not kidding. I will add that I loved living in this dorm and Campbell Hall next door.

Another student added,

I lived there for about one year. My experience was actually not that great. I am someone who sleeps light and I do not move, but I would wake up with bruises and scratches all over my arms. I had nightmares every night, and they were worse when my roommate was not sleeping in the same room as well. I think the strangest thing was when many of the girls woke up twice in the same night at the same exact time. I could not stay in my room without the lights on when I was alone. It is hard to explain, but there was something there that just wasn't right.

AZ Paranormal investigator Colleen Sulzer roomed in Morton Hall from 1996 to 1997. That cold winter brought on a heavy snowstorm with over three feet of snow, which shut down the school as well as most of the town. "It was the first time in sixty-five years the school had to close due to do weather issues. It was kind of eerie!"

Yes, it was much like that isolating December when Kathy was left all alone in the dormitory!

Colleen added, "There were always cold spots in the hallways of the first floor."

Twice, Colleen said, she and her roommate heard knocking at the door late at night and found nobody around. "The laundry room was always eerie—like someone was watching you. I hated going into that room! It always gave me the creeps!"

They say Kathy is not the only ghostly resident of Morton Hall. Students believe the spirits of two lovers haunt the basement. The tale of terror states that an amorous couple was making love in an underground tunnel that connects to the basement of Morton Hall. Supposedly, a water main in the tunnel happened to burst while the two lovers were busy inside. They were trapped by the rising waters and drowned. It is claimed their spirits still haunt the basement. Students report strange noises still rise from beneath the catacombs of Morton Hall. They say they hear laughter and moaning underneath the building, and something creates a disturbance by banging on the water pipes.

Truth or legend, the ghostly tale of Kathy is one that is most gossiped about among sorority sisters and the like—and the main reason none of the girls in Morton Hall want to stay behind during the holidays!

3

GILA COUNTY

GLOBE HIGH SCHOOL
460 NORTH WILLOW STREET
GLOBE, AZ 85501

Globe's early high school students attended classes at Central School, which was originally called Hill Street School. It was located near G Hill. As Globe's population grew, the early school became overcrowded, forcing the construction of a new, larger facility.

Construction for the building currently known as Globe High School began in 1913 and was completed in 1914. The updated school housed about 250 students from seventh grade to twelfth grade in a two-story building, complete with a basement.

The new school was constructed in a residential neighborhood close to the center of town, so the students could easily walk from their homes to school. With only a few motor vehicles in town, most students made the daily walk to school, scurried home for lunch and visited with their classmates on the school grounds before classes resumed.

In 1920, a third floor was designed by architects Trost and Trost to accommodate the growing number of junior high school students. Also at this time a cafeteria, a garage and locker rooms were added in the basement. There were additional accommodations for a caretaker who lived on site, and a nurse's office was added to the main floor.

The first Globe versus Miami football game was played in 1924. This started a major rivalry that led to the creation of the G and M Hills in each town in 1934, an attempt to curb vandalism at the schools, and the Copper Kettle trophy (cast in 1947). The competitive rivals' game was played on Thanksgiving until 1965, when Arizona's football season was changed to end on an earlier date.

The high school expanded into other nearby buildings in 1949, when the tennis courts made way for a gym and cafeteria. In 1956, a junior high school was built to provide more space for the needs of the high school. Science, music and shop wings were added in 1964. Globe High School was renovated in 1991, and today, it is one of the oldest buildings in Arizona continuously used for education. One of Globe's graduates, Rose Mofford, became Arizona's first woman governor.

And as can be expected, the century-old Globe High School has its share of ghosts! None of the spirits are known to be demonic or threatening. They are simply lingering to learn lessons in the historic mining town school.

Some former students and school employees have reported stories of a young boy, about seven years old, who wears a sailor suit and bounces a ball against the wall of the gym. They also speak of an elderly janitor who can still be heard "sweeping, sweeping with his broom." They also warned that if you are in the building late at night, you can hear the footsteps of someone walking around in a circle up on the second floor.

Stacy Waddell, a longtime teacher at Globe High School, shared a few of the ghost stories that have circulated over a couple decades.

> I have had several different ghostly encounters since I started working at the high school in 2003. During my second year of teaching, I was assigned to instruct yearbook and photography. So, I inherited two more classrooms: the yearbook office and the dark room, which consisted of three rooms. The front room of the dark room was more of a sitting room. It had a refrigerator and chairs inside it. Then there was the film room and the picture processing room. An old school radio, complete with an old-fashion dial, was inside the picture room. We could only tune in to about three radio stations. Several times, we would be in the room when, all of a sudden, the dial on the radio would start to scroll up and down the stations. Other times, the radio would just turn on or shut off by itself. I would bring my lunch every day and keep it in the refrigerator in the sitting room. I always drank a Diet Mtn Dew in the morning. Occasionally, I would forget my drink at home. But it seemed

Globe High School. *Author's collection.*

that every time I would absentmindedly go back into the room to get it, the refrigerator door and freezer door were found open.

One time when I reentered the room, the radio was blasting. Mind you, I had just been in the room, like, one minute, if that, before. Other experiences had by students included the old paper towel dispenser that we never used. It had a metal hand crank on it and would begin to crank while we were in the pitch dark trying to put the film on reel. We heard tapping feet, like the tapping of impatience, because the student couldn't get her film on the reel.

One spring break, the sprinklers on the front lawn were left on, and it flooded the dark room. We were devastated and had to renovate the room. Toward the end of the renovation, I only let the editors-in-chief work there. At this time, it was two female students. All of a sudden, they came running out of the room screaming. I asked what was going on, and they said there was a crazy noise like sizzling, crackling and popping. So, I went in there to check things out with them. We didn't hear any noises until we started to exit the room, when it actually made that sound again. It was a crazy sound! This time, we all ran out!

We would often stay late working on the yearbook, sometimes until 11:00 p.m. at night. During the late-night hours, we would hear doors slamming shut on the upper levels. We also heard the laughter of a child, and lights would sometimes flicker. In recent years, I have seen a little boy peeking in my room during class. I have seen him three times in a period of two years, and one of the times, another student saw him, too.

In 2009 or 2010, I told my friend about some of our experiences. She had friends in Tucson that ran an investigation group called Arizona Ghost to Ghost. We arranged for them to come to the school and do a paranormal investigation. I was able to get it approved by our principal at the time. We did not tell anyone else about the investigation so it would not to leak out to the students, who would probably try to prank us. The investigation team consisted of me, two other women and two gentlemen. At first, we decided to all stick together. We put cameras and recording devices to capture EVPs in the gym, since this was another hot spot where people had said they saw the little boy. We added more equipment in the basement and in the auditorium, where other frequent reports came from.

In the gym, we placed a basketball smack dab in the center of the gym. We decided to go to the auditorium and take some pictures. While in the auditorium, John, who is a medium, sensed a man in a tie was standing on the stage. I believe he said the man's name was Steven. He said Steven was a calm man. We all took several pictures and got some cool images of lights and some orbs. To me, one of the orbs looked to have a skull face in it. I used to keep the picture in my desk, but one day, it disappeared. We also heard a door slam shut on the second floor. About thirty minutes later, we returned to the gym. It was probably about 1:00 a.m. When we entered the gym, all of our equipment was different. The battery of the camera was dead, the EVP recording device was still running and the ball we placed in the center of the gym somehow ended up in the corner. We had propped open a door in the back of the gym with a chair to let in a little light, and that chair was on its side and the door was shut.

We grabbed the recorder and placed a new battery in the camera. We propped open the back door again and placed the basketball back in the center of the gym. The group decided to go into the cafeteria and get some water. We were in there for about five or so minutes listening to the EVPs. We all heard a child's voice that sounded like it said "hello" and then laughter. Freaked me out! Anyway, when we went back into the gym, we *walked into the same situation as before. The basketball was in the corner, the chair moved from the door and the camera battery was drained!*

This was the first investigation conducted at the high school. The following year, a school activity club was formed called the Paranormal Club. They made a couple attempts to stay and do an investigation—but, as you know, high school kids are skittish and play pranks on each other, so I don't feel like we got much out of any of those investigations.

Just last week, the teacher in the basement with me was sitting in her room with a student when a table flipped over on its side. She told me what happened and mentioned that a while back, she and her friend, who is a bit empathetic, were at the school, and her friend felt chills and had goosebumps. The friend said she felt the ghost's name was Steven.

BULLION PLAZA SCHOOL
150 NORTH PLAZA CIRCLE
MIAMI, AZ 85539

The Bullion School in the mining town of Miami, Arizona, is historically important, as it served Mexican Americans and dealt with school segregation in Arizona during the early half of the 1900s. The majestic Bullion Plaza School was housed in a two-story, reinforced concrete building located on the west end of Miami. The Neo-Classical Revival building was designed by the famed El Paso, Texas architecture firm of Trost and Trost and modeled after El Paso High School, a Neo-Classical Revival building designed by Henry Trost and built in 1916. The Bullion Plaza School was erected in 1923 and shares the Neo-Classical ornamentation that features the central clock, columns with elements from the Ionic order, cornices, pediments, a monumental portico with broad temple-like steps and a corniced parapet.

The school was active from 1923 until the end of the school year in 1994. Its doors were shut due to possible structural safety issues that made the building unsafe for students and the public. The Bullion Plaza School was listed in the National Register of Historic Places on November 27, 2000. Bullion Plaza was established as a segregated school, originally built for the neighboring Native and Mexican American children.

The segregation of Mexican American students was a common practice in Arizona public schools between 1900 and the early 1950s. This was the same period in which Bullion Plaza school served as a segregated school for Miami's children. School administrators at the time believed vocational training schools were needed for Mexican American students because of a perceived idea that they may not have the ability to perform well in traditional scholastic subjects.

The formal segregation of Mexican American students in Arizona schools persisted until the early 1950s, when a court decision forced local school districts to drop the practice. This occurred alongside the movement to end the segregation of the Black population, but the two movements were largely separate. Both, however, had their origins in increasing actions from minority parents, who showed that their children's schools were not only separate but also inferior, despite the claim of educators and school administrators that segregation was based on the theory of "separate but equal."

Today, the Bullion Plaza building is a historic museum that houses collections and artifacts that reflect the history of the town. Some of the historic relics from Miami and the surrounding area still hold the energy of their previous owners. The building also houses old war/medical memorabilia and historical cultural exhibits. There have been reports of many unexplained paranormal phenomena throughout the building, and these have contributed to numerous ghost stories surrounding the museum and former school.

The second floor is said to be haunted by a malevolent male spirit, which has been known to frighten the staff and some of the visitors. One of the commonly reported apparitions on the first floor, or the main floor, is that of a beautiful woman in a flowing white dress. She has appeared to staff during the daytime hours and late at night.

A local said, "I have seen a small child, the woman ghost, and male figure in this building on several occasions. My sister has seen them, too. This all happened sometime between 1996 and 1999, when the school was still closed for restoration and preservation."

Aside from being a school that educated children from first to eighth grade, Bullion Plaza was around through polio outbreaks, tuberculosis and an attempted murder in its lobby, and it is reported that some of the school's children were punished there for speaking their Native language.

Paranormal tour group AZ Ghost Adventures have experienced orbs, objects being moved, voices, flashlight-on-command activity, K2 meter hits and other equipment activity in the former school. They also believe

The former Bullion Plaza School. *Author's collection.*

there is an active dark spirit energy in the basement that one of their tour guests photographed. Most members of the museum staff refuse to enter the basement alone. They feel the dark, cemented storage area may be hanging on to dark energies left behind by unknown intruders who frequented the catacombs when the building was empty and unattended.

After I investigated the Bullion Plaza Building, along with fellow investigators, I feel the building holds in heavy residual energy that plays out acts of violence over and over again. Although there were never any deaths that occurred on the school's grounds, the schoolchildren, teachers and staff were firsthand witnesses to horrifying and vicious attacks!

Miami resident Aurora Serna, eighteen, and Joe Berumen, twenty-one, were married sometime in December 1937. They opted to live in the Live Oaks addition with Berumen's parents and family. This arrangement seemed to go along quite well until something went terribly wrong on the afternoon of November 21, 1938.

An argument evolved, and within minutes, the young bride dashed out of the house screaming as her father-in-law, Mr. Pastor Berumen, chased her down the road waving a thirty-inch-long, three-edge Moroccan bayonet!

Aurora quickly ran to the safety of Bullion Plaza School, where she entered through the right rear door screaming, "Save me! Save me!"

W.L. Longan, the principal of the school, was at work in his office when Mrs. Berumen ran into the hallway. Berumen, her father-in-law, was in hot pursuit. Principal Longan rushed out into the hall and attempted to stop Berumen but missed when he swung with his fist and lost his balance. Longan hurried into an adjoining room, where he found a club to act as a weapon.

Pastor Berumen followed Aurora into the classroom of Miss Elma Eckstein, where he drove the bayonet into Aurora's right shoulder. The blade came out through her left breast. Longan said Berumen was attempting to pull the bayonet from his daughter-in-law's shoulder when Longan entered the room. The man then climbed out an open window and fled.

Distraught, Aurora Berumen slowly pulled the dagger out and threw it across the room. It slid across the floor and struck a pupil. The point of the bayonet passed through his shoe but did not damage the boy's feet.

Aurora Berumen received treatment at Inspiration Hospital for her stab wound. She was then sent home, where she soon recovered. Her father-in-

Bullion Plaza Cultural Center and Museum. *Author's collection.*

law, Pastor Berumen, was captured in the hills three miles west of Miami and arrested in connection with the stabbing. An assault charge with an attempt to commit murder was filed, and Pastor Berumen later served a short prison sentence.

Can you imagine the looks that were given by the students when their mothers asked, "How was school today?"

To add to the unexplained energies found around Bullion School, back in September 1925, Jose Gonzales stabbed his wife five times with a pocketknife and then turned the weapon on himself, inflicting a severe neck wound while schoolchildren of the Bullion Plaza School looked on. The woman rushed to the Miami Inspiration dispensary suffering only flesh wounds and recovered while her husband had only a fighting chance to survive.

Or could it be additional residual energy from the free-for-all fight that occurred on the Bullion Plaza grounds late one evening. In the fight, a woman received a deep gash on her arm, and her companion suffered a scalp wound supposedly from flying rocks.

It is also said that, in the 1970s, a gentleman was found dead inside the old school on the staircase that leads down from the second floor. Is this the gentleman many have heard moaning on recording devices? Perhaps he is seeking answers about his untimely demise.

With a structure so active, it's no wonder Bullion Plaza is one of the most haunted locations in Arizona.

NOFTSGER HILL SCHOOL
(MOST RECENTLY THE NOFTSGER HILL INN)
425 NORTH STREET
GLOBE, AZ 85501

The Noftsger Hill Inn sits high on a hill overlooking the city of Globe and dates to 1907, when it was known as the North Globe School. As miners flocked to work in Globe's copper mines, a larger school became necessary to serve the needs of the growing community; this much larger building was established to fill that need. In 1917, the front half of the existing structure was added, and its name was changed to Noftsger Hill School, after Globe businessman A.N. Noftsger (the hill it sits on bore his name first). Noftsger made his living by supplying local miners and their families with a resource more precious than Globe's silver or copper: water. (He had purchased the area's water rights.) The school that bore Noftsger's name educated many generations of children until 1981, when the schoolhouse closed its doors for more than just the summer. Here, school was finally out for good. The school's most famous student is former Arizona governor Rose Mofford (1988–91).

The building sat vacant for ten years. New ownership and renovations changed this landmark school into a bright, spacious and charming bed-and-breakfast. Now, visitors can reserve one of six classrooms and enjoy fabulous views of the Old Dominion Mine or a breathtaking view of the city of Globe. (Rooms in the front of the building provide views of the Pinal Mountains and the town of Globe. The rooms in the back look out onto the historic Old Dominican Mine.)

The former Noftsger Hill Inn has always been the leader of my top ten haunted weekend getaways in the desert metropolis of Phoenix. Only ninety minutes away, Globe offers a higher altitude and a lower temperature. The town is also said to be quite haunted due to its rough-and-tumble days as a turn-of-the-century mining town. But as the town became civilized, a school to educate the children was needed.

The stately Noftsger Hill School operated from 1907 to 1981, educating generations of Globe children. Some of these former students often visited their old school for small class reunions and gatherings with friends and classmates. And some of the school chums who frequent the two-story building come from the far-away spirit world.

There seems to be a few ghosts in the old building that decided to stay after school was over. Ghost hunters found the quiet bed-and-breakfast the perfect spot for capturing EVPs and encountering a spirit or two. It is the perfect location to reserve all the rooms at the inn and enjoy a weekend with a group of paranormal investigators.

Four women made the trip up to Globe for a mid-week stay (school days) at the Noftsger Hill Inn. Their goal was to hopefully photograph apparitions or get audio recordings of the schoolchildren. Students' distant voices are often heard in the building, as though they are being projected from another dimension. Footsteps are heard in the hallways of the inn where students move between the now-vacant classrooms. Disembodied voices echo in the old cloak halls, now converted into modern bathrooms. Many guests search for hidden messages written on the old chalkboards that still line the classrooms.

Noftsger Hill School stands quiet today. *Author's collection.*

The guests asked the inn's former innkeeper, the delightful Rosalie Ayala, if there had been any recent antics of the mischievous children. She smiled and recalled a story told by two guests who had checked out a few weeks earlier.

"The ladies had been out sightseeing and shopping during the day and stopped for dinner in Globe," Rosalie recalled. "They brought back a bottle of fine wine to their room and placed it in an ice bucket. They poured two glasses of wine and recorked the bottle. A short while later, the cork popped from the wine bottle. It landed several feet away from the ice bucket. The startled ladies laughed the episode off—but when it happened the second time that evening, they decided it might be a good idea to leave a light on!"

After hearing the story of the recent guests, the foursome gathered in the dark around a table and began to call in the spirited schoolchildren. Activities on their EMF meters, K-2s and Mel Meters were null to none. One of the ladies whipped out a pair of dowsing rods and began asking a series of yes or no questions in the darkness. The spirit of a former student, a little girl in the second grade, responded to the conversation by directing the movement of the dowsing rods to the left and right. Their young contact did not stay very long, and soon, their after-school activities came to an end.

After breakfast the following morning, it was time to pack up and head back down to Phoenix. The women stood talking to their hostess for several minutes until one of the ladies happened to glance over her left shoulder. Out of the corner of her eye, she saw a small child dash out of the room the group had been staying in (room 3), go around the corner and run up the staircase toward the small restroom on the mid-landing. She chuckled to herself. After all, it was a middle-of-the-week school day, and classes would have been in session at 10:00 a.m. It was just another endless day of summer school for the spirits at the Noftsger Hill School.

On another occasion, paranormal investigators Megan Taylor and Debe Branning booked room 2 on the first floor. "We carefully unloaded our bags of paranormal equipment and cameras on a table in the room. Almost immediately, strange things began to happen. We sat down in a couple of rocking chairs in the center of the room to plan our strategy for the night. Megan glanced over to a leather reading chair and saw the apparition of an elderly, partially bald, white-haired man with long sideburns leaning over, as if he was listening to our conversation. Then he faded away."

"We also saw the shadow of a youngster glide down the wall near the chalkboards and linger in a corner for some time. The corridor walls of the bed-and-breakfast were lined with classroom photographs that were once captured on the front steps of Noftsger Hill School. Megan recognized the visitor in our room from one the photographs. He appeared to be a former schoolteacher or principal."

"Later, I was chatting near the edge of Megan's bed when a very strange event occurred right before my eyes. I glanced down to see a small, black fuzzy mass about the size of a child's fist emerge from under the bed, punch the outside of my right foot and retract back under the bed. I quickly dove to the ground on my hands and knees to see what was under the bed but found nothing."

The MVD Ghostchasers held a paranormal workshop at the Noftsger Hill Inn in January 2009. They had every inch of the building covered for a thorough investigation, so there was no way any paranormal activity could slip past them. They held several EVP sessions throughout the night. They were able to debunk some of the previous reports of unexplained voices and lights in room 1. There is an electrical power box connected to the outer wall of that particular room that projects an extremely high EMF reading near the bed and sitting area. This could cause anxiety and the feeling of being watched.

Ghost hunters have captured EVPs of footsteps walking across the inn's wooden floor and, of course, the faraway voices of children. They have photographed strange balls of lights on camcorders rolling during the night, usually around 3:00 a.m. Guests have also heard the faint voices of teachers instructing their classrooms.

On Saturday, April 26, 2014, FOTOS (Friends of the Other Side) had the opportunity to conduct an overnight investigation at the historic Noftsger Hill Inn. They chose to stay in room 3 for the weekend, since they had heard there was activity associated with this room. Once they were checked in and had set up trigger objects for an experiment, they decided to sit quietly in the room to try to catch a read on the room and the rest of the building. During this quiet time, Jen, a team member of FOTOS, was repeatedly firmly touched, like someone was poking her or pushing on her. Jill, another member of FOTOS, could see the finger impression in Jen's sleeved arm.

After Carolee Jacson, the leader of FOTOS, introduced herself to the spirit with her usual introduction of peace, love, respect and asking permission, she was immediately approached by a young female spirit; she was about four and a half feet tall with bobbed blond hair. Carolee asked her name, and she said, "Evelyn."

"Can you repeat your name for me?"

"Evelyn."

"Evelyn, you went to school here?"

"Yes."

Then Evelyn began repeating "five, five, five," to which Carolee asked if she was five years old. No. Fifth grade? Yes. That is when a young, thin male with tousled brown hair stepped forward to correct Evelyn by saying "eight" several times, which Evelyn began adamantly denying. She insisted on five. And then Evelyn said, "Paul likes to push."

"Push to hurt?"

"No, push!" Evelyn showed Carolee one finger poking or firmly pushing. In the info-relay, you could sense Evelyn enjoyed telling Carolee about Paul and what she determined was naughty behavior. Carolee asked the young man his name, and he confirmed it was Paul and that he was eight years old. Paul said Evelyn likes to tattle and move things. Evelyn said Paul likes pushing people. Carolee asked if Paul was pushing on Jen and was told "yes." It seems Evelyn and Paul like to hang out on the lower level of the inn and will make their presence known to the innkeeper and visitors. Evelyn doesn't hesitate to peek around doors and furniture and has made herself at home. Paul tends to be shyer and follows Evelyn around quite a bit.

After an eventful night of sounds, shadows and more visits from Evelyn and Paul, the FOTOS members also had a meeting with the third- and fourth-grade teacher from the 1940s who taught upstairs for a long time.

The doorknob on the room's door closed and latched. The door rattled like someone was trying to enter the room. The hand towel in the bathroom would not stay on the towel bar, and Carolee observed it being tugged off.

The four members of the FOTOS team went to sleep and woke up ready to do some research on the school's former students and teachers. (Schoolteachers is plural because Carolee was up earlier for a solo dowsing rod session when she met a male teacher who taught in room 2, died while school was in session and was concerned for the kids he left behind.)

While waiting for breakfast, the four FOTOS members meandered around the downstairs lobby, checking out the place more thoroughly, looking for information on the spirits they had encountered. Carolee was at one end of the room, where she had caught the spirits of four girls hushing themselves by the girls' bathroom. She was quite surprised she could hear them when, all of a sudden, Carolee heard Wendy and Jen call, "Carolee! Evelyn is here! Her picture is on the wall!" Carolee dashed to where her excited friends were standing and pointing. There was Evelyn standing in a classroom group picture. "I recognized her immediately."

Another event that Jen and Carolee witnessed in real time was the self-illuminating light that had been reportedly seen by other visitors on the lower level. They saw the light form; Jen had her camera, so she started to take pictures of it. The light moved toward them, softly skipping across the floor and furnishings until it disappeared after sitting on the table for a few seconds.

Carolee recalled in her notes: "Picture 1: light appears near floor, Picture 2: moves toward us on floor level, Picture 3: moved up to piano, Picture 4: seen on table next to piano, Picture 5: light disappears."

On another occasion, Kenton Moore remembered seeing a similar moving light. "I woke up in the middle of the night to use the bathroom. After I had finished, I opened the bathroom door to head back to bed. A speeding ball of light flew over my shoulder and across the room. Then it suddenly disappeared." Earlier in the evening he had placed his truck keys on a dresser but could not find them before he settled down for the night. He searched everywhere and finally decided to continue the hunt in the morning. To his surprise, in the morning, the keys were back on the dresser in the exact same spot he had placed them in the night before!

And don't forget all those children who appear in the school building from time to time who love to play pranks on the guests.

Meleana Tomoded once visited the former bed-and-breakfast with her late mother. "I kept hearing children playing in the middle of the night. It sounded like they were outside on the playground, and it woke me up. I thought it was just a dream until I opened my eyes. I kept listening but drifted off to sleep. I woke up at dawn, and there were no children playing outside or in the building. We were staying in the Fiesta Room."

The Noftsger Hill Inn was once one of the most sought-out weekend getaways. Its owners would often urge, "Sleep in class at the Noftsger Hill Inn." (And we never had to clean the chalkboards and erasers.)

Of course, there is still the urban legend the children of Globe like to share about the ghosts of Noftsger Hill School. They say the ghost of a mean teacher still walks the hallways, and they claim the bones of the evil teacher are buried in the basement!

MYSTERY OF THE OLD STRAWBERRY SCHOOLHOUSE
9277 FOSSIL CREED ROAD
STRAWBERRY, AZ 85544

In April 2013, the adventuresome teams of Cemetery Crawl 8 traveled across Arizona to historic and haunted cemeteries in the central area of the state. The group traveled the back highways and discovered the beauty of the towns along Highway 87, including Payson, Pine and Strawberry. Aside from visiting local cemeteries, the teams were instructed to visit various historic monuments and buildings along the scenic roads.

Around 1884, the families living near the Strawberry Valley in the Arizona Territory petitioned the county school superintendent to establish a school. The petition was granted, and District 33 in the Strawberry Valley was

Strawberry Schoolhouse. *Wikimedia.*

established. But there was a local dispute over where that school building was to be constructed. The problem was resolved when a group of cowboys used a calf rope and counted the number of lengths between the Hicks-Duncan Cabin on the west end of the valley and the Peach Cabin on the east end. They retraced their steps to the midpoint. It was there the one-room log cabin school was built and still stands today. It is one of the oldest standing schoolhouses in Arizona.

There was an eighty-year-old mystery involving the old schoolhouse that haunted the minds and souls of former teachers and students for many years. Local historians state that in 1886, pieces of chalk began to disappear, one after another. Chalk was not easy to come by in those days and neither was the blackboard eraser that turned up missing, too. Then one day, the teacher's gold watch disappeared during recess. She had left it untended on her desk while everyone enjoyed a sunny afternoon outdoors.

Suspecting a thief among her students, the teacher kept the entire class after school, and each student was interrogated individually. The teacher had the class recite the Ten Commandments over and over again. She even sent notes home to the parents. Nobody ever confessed to the thievery. The schoolteacher eventually left the Strawberry Valley area, the missing items not found.

Later, in 1965, the citizens of the Strawberry Valley area campaigned to raise money to restore the abandoned Strawberry Schoolhouse and open it as a museum. When the carpenters climbed up into the attic to set new rafters for a new roof, they made an amazing discovery and found the answer to the eighty-year-old secret. Up in the attic was an old pack rat's nest containing bits of glitter and glass, hairpins and coins. Among the treasure were pieces of white chalk, an eraser and a lady's gold watch!

Is the old schoolhouse haunted? Stop by to pay a visit and see for yourself. And don't be a dunce—remember donations are always welcome!

The Strawberry Schoolhouse is open from mid-May to mid-October on Saturdays from 10:00 a.m. to 4:00 p.m. and on Sundays from 12:00 p.m. to 4:00 p.m. From June 15 to August 6, the school is open on Fridays and Mondays.

4

MARICOPA COUNTY

CHANDLER HIGH SCHOOL
350 NORTH ARIZONA AVENUE
CHANDLER, AZ 85225

The community of Chandler was founded by Dr. A.J. Chandler on May 17, 1912. Chandler High School is one of the oldest high schools in Arizona. The original high school opened its doors in September 1914, just two years after the city of Chandler was founded and Arizona declared statehood, both in 1912. Breaking ground for the current building (complete with a small gymnasium) began in 1921. As it is one of the oldest parts of the building, it is affectionately referred as Old Main. The building was constructed in a Classical Revival style by architects Allison and Allison. Orville A. Bell designed the current gymnasium in 1939. Both structures were placed in the National Register of Historic Places in 2007. The school's name comes from the city's founder, Dr. Alexander John "A.J." Chandler, a local veterinary surgeon.

Old Main seems to be the hottest site on campus for paranormal activity. Voices and ghostly apparitions are experienced in the hallways on the second floor of the English building. Paranormal sightings and disembodied voices are still experienced in the north wing of the historic building.

One student said, "I go Chandler High School, and it is haunted. Sometimes, you can see a person looking out the window on the top floor

Chandler High School entrance. *Author's collection.*

of Old Main. Teachers say there is no basement in Old Main, but I found it—unfortunately, the door was locked. I saw a set of stairs going down, but then it went black, and I swear there was another door with a lock on it. I'm scared that the ghost might get angry one day with all the stories!"

Another concerned student added, "I just started going to Chandler High. My friend and I were heading to English class, and we entered through the door to Old Main on the far left. After we went inside, we saw two doors under the stairwell. One door was installed with a small window. I decided to take a quick peek, and I could see stairs going down, and boy, did it look creepy as hell! I noticed the door was the only one that had a different kind of lock on the outside door."

The number of people who have had paranormal experiences in the school is surprisingly high, and they include teaching staff members, students, parents, administrators, visitors and custodians—both former and current. The activity seems to be more or less focused on the second floor of the school's north wing, which is noted as the oldest building on the school's campus.

One teacher felt the presence of a spirit standing nearby while she used the restroom in the faculty lounge. Another instructor witnessed a ghost enter the school's auditorium, pause for a moment and then quickly exit through another door.

A janitor who has been employed at Chandler High School for almost thirty years admits he has encountered a male apparition five or six times in the hallways of the English building. Apparently, the building is so haunted

Above: Chandler High School English building. *Courtesy of Cindy Lee.*

Left: The Chandler High School window where a ghost is seen. *Courtesy of Cindy Lee.*

that at least one of the custodians has refused to clean it after they endured a paranormal encounter there.

MVD Ghostchaser Cindy Lee recalled attending a high school basketball game in the gymnasium in late 1969 or early 1970. Cindy was not a student at the high school but often attended events there with her friends. During halftime, the group of friends stepped outside to get a bit of fresh air and continued socializing. Cindy wandered near the windows of the English building. Glancing upward, she noticed the figure of a man standing at a second-floor window with a soothing blue aura surrounding him.

"It reminded me of the color of the ocean," Cindy recalled. "I was looking high into the window and could only see his body from the waist up. I just remember it was a beautiful shade of blue. I kept watching until it finally faded away. It was then I learned I had observed the famous 'blue ghost' of Chandler High School."

GILBERT ELEMENTARY SCHOOL, OR THE GILBERT HISTORY MUSEUM
10 SOUTH GILBERT ROAD
GILBERT, AZ 85296

Stories that the Gilbert Museum building is haunted surfaced in the early 1980s, when a former Gilbert Unified School District superintendent kept his office where the gift shop is presently located. The museum building, formerly Gilbert Elementary School, opened in 1913 as the third home of Gilbert's first elementary school. The need for schools grew as the population in Gilbert soared with all the cotton manufacturing, farming and ranching in the area. A good education became a must for the local children.

The Mission-style school building consisted of four classrooms, two offices and an auditorium with a full basement below the auditorium. Four steps led up to a large porch area that was highlighted by a bell above the east-facing middle entrance. There were two other entrances: one facing north and one facing south.

In 1977, the school building was closed for classroom duty, and in 1982, it became the Gilbert Historical Museum. Guests can still walk on the original wooden floors and examine the old slate chalkboards that line the walls of one of the classroom settings.

Gilbert Elementary School, also known as the Gilbert Historical Museum. *Author's collection.*

One of the building's haunting tales centers on a former school nurse who once occupied an office in the building. She is said to be responsible for much of the building's ghostly activity. Museum staff have heard floorboards creaking and furniture sliding across the floor.

There is also a lot of activity in the basement area. Groups like the West Coast Ghost and Paranormal Society have investigated the building on several occasions.

Other paranormal teams have reported hearing a girl's voice humming a song and the feeling that they walked through a mass of hanging cobwebs. While exploring the museum, Megan Taylor and Debe Branning felt as though a spirit from the past was keeping a watchful eye on them for their entire visit—they were just curious.

The Phoenix Arizona Paranormal Society (PAPS) did an investigation in October 2014. They interviewed museum staff and volunteers to learn what they had heard and seen over the years. One volunteer said they once heard equipment, like a crank, running in the area of the blacksmith shop. At the time, he was in the building conducting his own investigation with a friend. They were the only two people on the premises.

Museum docent Susan Hoff noted that she had heard a female voice greet her with a "hello" when she arrived for her morning shift. She and other employees have also heard sighs and soft whispers. She believes there are two spirits that have made the former schoolhouse their home. One is a male, and the other is a child the staff has nicknamed Kate.

Another longtime museum volunteer once organized the storage area in the basement of the building, where surplus museum items are kept. He said he had to move a large doll from the main display floor to the basement after one of the female docents began noting its head was constantly turned in various positions—almost like it was moving to glance in different directions. After the doll was positioned in a glass display cabinet, its head finally fell off all together. Rather than allow the doll to frighten the visiting guests with its blank Victorian stare, museum volunteers decided the basement was the best place to keep it.

The museum volunteer was also asked to move two mannequins to the basement to be placed in storage. The volunteer gently placed them on the seat of an old barber chair that once sat in Gilbert's renowned Ray's Barber Shop. When the worker came into the building after a long weekend, he found both mannequins dismantled, their legs and arms tossed about the basement. He placed the troubled pieces into a lawn bag and hurled them into the alley dumpster. "I don't think Ray the barber was too pleased with the mannequins disturbing his treasured barber chair."

The PAPS team did several comprehensive investigations of the museum, focusing on the basement, where the spirits played with the team's paranormal equipment. Their devices picked up a lot of movement in the area, and the team recorded various levels of energy on their EMF meters. After finding a quiet area, the team asked several questions to learn who remained in the old schoolhouse. They were rewarded with recordings of disembodied voices and the sound of swishing skirts, as though someone was walking nearby.

The museum is chock-full of the history of early Gilbert, Arizona, and its early schools. Energy radiates off many of the relics, and who knows, perhaps "Mr. Manny Quinn" is still searching for the missing display models he once lost his head over. But be careful, this spirit may be "armed" and dangerous!

HIGHLAND JUNIOR HIGH
6915 EAST GUADALUPE ROAD
MESA, AZ 85212

The locker room at Gilbert's Highland Junior High, built in 1997, is allegedly haunted by a young girl who flushes the toilets, turns on the blow dryers and bangs on the locker doors. School officials claim she is not a former student of the school, which opened in 1998, but perhaps a little girl who was killed on the farmland the school was built on. Urban legend states the girl was accidently killed when a tractor driven by her father ran over her. There is no documented evidence of who the girl might be, but most students and alumni have given her the name Lily.

One former student reported, "When I was in a PE class in seventh grade, I needed to go back to the locker room to grab a pencil. All alone, I went to my locker and tried to unlock it. No success. All of a sudden, the lights flickered on and off…and then the dryers and a shower turned on. I decided I didn't really the pencil and got the hell out of there."

A brave eighth-grader noted,

I was changing in the locker room—alone—and my friend was not there to open the combination lock to the locker. I had a hard time remembering the combination to her lock—but I finally got it! By the time I was able to get the locker open, the students had already gone to do spike ball or some other activities. I changed and went to the bathroom to wash my face and hands. As I started to wash up, the lights began to flicker, and I thought the power was going out or something. After washing my face and hands, I started to leave, but once I put my hands on the door, I heard the toilet flush. No one was in there with me. I even turned around to double check—and I was definitely alone! I ran out of their telling myself "Nope!" I told my friends about the event that just happened, and some of them believed me and some didn't.

Another student said,

When I attended Highland Junior High, I had early morning practices for sports. We were instructed to enter through the unlit girls' locker room to go to the gym. I went in alone, and there was music playing from the stereo. This was not so creepy until I started listening to the heavy metal song that was blaring with scary lyrics—quite different from the pop tunes the PE

Highland Junior High School in Mesa. *Author's collection.*

teachers usually played. As I walked through, a locker door slammed from the back of the locker room. I turned to look, but nothing was there except one emergency light that showed all the locker doors open. This was weird, because most people lock their lockers! Then a hand dryer turned on, and I ran out of there—fast! I never believed in the tall tale until then!

And the reports continue! "So, once, in PE class, I had to head back to the locker room because I forgot my pedometer. I went back into the locker room to where the rack of pedometers hung. Suddenly, the hand dryers went off, and I heard a loud squeaking noise. At first, I thought it was no big deal because perhaps somebody was in the bathroom. I grabbed my pedometer and left, but the whole time, nobody came out of the locker room, which made me begin to freak out!"

Are there motion sensors? Is it Lily the ghost? It is enough to keep these students from holding any extracurricular activities in this locker room!

MYSTERY SCHOOL 911 CALL
GILBERT SCHOOL

On Halloween night 2020, two friends, Megan Taylor and Raven Wright, wanted to do something scary to celebrate the holiday. They had heard of a popular app that could be downloaded to one's cellphone. It was raved about all over YouTube for providing "frightening experiences." The app was called Randonautica. The ladies downloaded the app, and then, under the search options, they typed "find a ghost." They hit enter, and the app then gave them coordinates and driving directions to "find a ghost," as requested. It was very late that night, close to midnight. They got in their car and drove to the location the app provided. To their surprise, the app had directed them to an "undisclosed Gilbert High School" in Gilbert, Arizona. They slowly exited their car and approached the front of the high school. They stood outside the building for a few minutes and waited. Admittedly, they did sense a spooky atmosphere, but nothing else happened. They shrugged their shoulders, laughed it off and went home.

In 2023, Megan and I met with a few other paranormal enthusiasts, Colleen Sulzer, Carolee Jackson and Pete and Robbin Jerich, to attend a guest lecture at the AZ Heritage Center at Papago Park in Tempe. One group of guest speakers were Navajo Rangers. The second round of speakers, USP-PD, was a group of retired police officers who investigate paranormal and UFO-related incidents that have been reported by first responders.

Megan recalled the lecture.

> As the second group started their lecture, one of the locations they reported was the "undisclosed Gilbert High School." It seems that one night, a 911 call was placed from within the school. The 911 operator reported that a young woman had called in. When asked the nature of the emergency, the young woman said, "I'm scared." Fearing the worst, officers were dispatched to the school. When they arrived, the interior lights of the school were all off. They accessed the building and approached the front desk. The security lights, which are motion activated, came on. Once activated, they remain on for twenty minutes. The officers stated their response time was merely eight minutes. When they looked at the area of the front desk, the telephone was found off the hook. How had someone come to the front desk and used the telephone without tripping the security lights?

The officers searched the building, and when they walked the hallway that led to the offices, they felt a rush of wind blow by, as if someone had run past them! After a thorough search, the officers never found anyone hiding in the building.

Megan added, "When the USP-PD paranormal investigators Marianne Robb and Dave Rich followed up on the incident, they checked to see if the school had a history of being haunted. It did not. They did interview a school employee to ask if they had noticed anything unusual, since the incident report mentioned that something seemed to have rushed out past them near the front office."

Perhaps it was the employee and not the building that was haunted. Theory says that sometimes, a spirit attachment can follow a person for years and years. After a move to a new location, the haunting may stop for a short time, but eventually, the spirit can locate the haunted soul and follow them through this life once again.

Later, the USP-PD investigators went back to relisten to the recorded 911 call again. After analyzing the recording and listening to it multiple times, they realized the young woman was not saying "I'm scared." She was saying, "I scare!"

This may explain why the Randonautica app took Megan and Raven to the school that eerie Halloween night.

DEER VALLEY HIGH SCHOOL
18424 NORTH FIFTY-FIRST AVENUE
GLENDALE, AZ 85308

Deer Valley High School is a public high school located in Glendale, Arizona. It is part of the Deer Valley Unified School District. The school opened its doors for the first time in 1980 with an enrollment of 750 students. Today, the campus is housed on more than sixty acres and has a current enrollment of about 2,200 students. Renovations completed in 2011 were the first major overhauls done to the school since its 1980 construction and may have stirred up the location's paranormal activity.

Phoenix is certainly not short of haunted buildings, but it seems to have an overabundance of a certain type of property: schools! One of the many schools to feature a ghost is Deer Valley High School, where students apparently run into a male ghost with some degree of regularity. He has been nicknamed Dewey (some students call him Dwex), and he most often appears in the school auditorium. Who he is and why he is there remain unknown, but many students and teachers have had unexplained encounters with Dewey.

He is rumored to peer down from the auditorium's catwalk during the assemblies and then suddenly disappear into thin air. He has been known to tamper with the electrical equipment, lights and the projectors, and students often hear his disembodied voice. Others say they have simply felt his presence in the auditorium or feel that they are being watched, while others describe hearing faint crying and moaning.

Some students have shared the experiences they had with Dewey. One student said, "I was working one night in the booth where the sound and lighting are controlled for musicals, plays and dance concerts. All of my friends had headed backstage while another guy and I stood by the main staircase. I looked over to the right near a dark hallway leading to the prop room and the stairs to the catwalk. I witnessed a shadowy male figure walk up the stairs!"

One night, another teen who was visiting the campus started calling Dewey's name from his car parked across the street from the school. "I felt strange, and my heart dropped in fear. I kept provoking him, saying, 'You're fake!' And suddenly, I saw a teen in a white T-shirt and black hair run past the back of my car from the rearview mirror. That was the last time I ever messed with Dewey."

Stories of how Dewey died range from a love story gone wrong to a job gone wrong, in which a construction worker fell off the scaffolding while the school was being built. Another student who encountered the spirit during choir practice in the auditorium noted, "He is kind of creepy, but Dewey is pretty harmless." Without a doubt, Dewey is still having fun at school and soaring with the Skyhawks.

GHOSTS OF DESERT EDGE HIGH SCHOOL
15778 WEST YUMA ROAD
GOODYEAR, AZ 85338

The MVD Ghostchasers were invited by one of the instructors at Desert Edge High School in Goodyear, Arizona, to take another look at the school's reportedly haunted auditorium. The high school was constructed in 2002 and is home to the Scorpions.

Todd VanHooser, who once organized a yearly Laughing Moon Paracon for high school students, shared some of the noted haunts of the assembly hall building.

For many years, there have been reports of lights going on and off, balls of light seen in the crow's nests, temperature drops [cold spots] and cellphones ringing all at the exact same time from no number. People in restroom stalls hearing footsteps and faucets turning on in the bathroom only to discover no one else was in there. They hear static voices over the mikes during play rehearsals, and there have been several eyewitness accounts of a young girl in the crow's nest, and a woman who says, "Excuse me, I'm looking for my daughter. Can you please help me?" This last was seen by a student three years ago and former janitorial staff about four years ago. A janitor saw the woman wearing an older style of dress walk through a wall after their encounter. Another witness saw the woman fade away and disappear. I've experienced the strange lights going on and off personally, although there appears no rhyme or reason behind it.

Desert Edge High School in Buckeye. *Courtesy of the Desert Edge Facebook page.*

Research gathered by Ginger Mason of Verde Valley Spirit Seekers showed the area where the school is built was once the southern tip of Camp 53, one of the camps built for migrant workers who tended the area's fields of cotton. This cotton was used in the nearby Goodyear Tire and Rubber Company in 1929. The workers and their families lived in small adobe and wood houses.

Each camp was like a small community, where the workers lived and helped one another. There were no hospitals close at hand, so most of the children were born at home in the camps. Many people perished from accidents and diseases in the camp confines, and some of the women were left behind to care for and tend to the families while most went to the fields. Many of the families' dead were buried in unmarked graves at the old Goodyear Farms Cemetery a few miles northeast of the school.

The Desert Edge Workshop/Investigation was attended by about fourteen students and fourteen local paranormal investigators—members of a variety of longtime operational, ghost investigating groups. Armed with several brands of EMF meters, cameras, audio recorders and various voice boxes, the group met in front of the auditorium stage.

Everyone received handouts and had an opportunity to make a small protection packet of sea salt and rosemary to repel negativity. Then the assembly was divided into four smaller investigating groups, combining students with veteran ghost investigators. These groups did three to four rotations through the various haunted spots in the auditorium.

The teams investigated the crow's nests, or the upstairs area of the theater that houses the spotlights for stage productions. The spirit of a young girl is often spotted there, looking down at the seats in the auditorium. The various investigation groups came up with possible names for the spirits, like Frank and Maria, with the use of the ghost voice boxes, which are designed to make communication with those beyond possible.

Some groups found the backstage area active with the sounds of footsteps and banging, while others felt a presence in the dressing room bathrooms. Shadowy figures were seen darting here and there, keeping a watchful eye on the auditorium.

A large closet area for storing props and stage equipment has been the site where students often hear conversations without a source. One of the investigators made contact with a gentleman high above the group along the wall, as though he had been trapped in time on a lift or some type of ladder. Perhaps there was some sort of accident during construction of the school, or perhaps the mishap dates even farther back, during the time of cotton farming and tire manufacturing.

LEHI SCHOOL, OR THE MESA HISTORICAL MUSEUM
2345 NORTH HORNE STREET
MESA, AZ 85203

The old Lehi School was built in 1913 and is the oldest standing school building in Mesa, Arizona. It is known for its modern, Mission/Spanish Revival architectural style. Lehi is now a distinct community within Mesa, Arizona, although Lehi existed prior to the founding of Mesa. Lehi was annexed into its much larger neighbor in 1970 and is now the northern limit of central Mesa. Lehi is adjacent to the Salt River to the north and the Consolidated Canal to the south.

Properties of note in the Lehi area include the Old Lehi School, which was placed in the National Register of Historic Places in August 2001. It is currently the home of the Mesa Historical Museum.

The structure originally built as the Lehi School auditorium was constructed as a Works Progress Administration (WPA) project in 1936. Located on the east side of North Horne Street and east of Lehi Road, the

Lehi School Museum in Mesa. *Author's collection.*

Lehi School's auditorium. *Author's collection.*

building is now also part of the Mesa Historical Museum complex. It was so well built that it was designated the community bomb shelter during the Cold War. Later, due to its sturdy construction, when the building was no longer needed, it was deemed too costly to tear down. For this reason, the school and auditorium remain intact and are popular sites for local visitors.

Guests were encouraged to participate on a ghost tour of the old Lehi School between 6:00 p.m. and 10:00 p.m. on October 23, 2010, just in time for the Halloween season. They were instructed to bring their flashlights and cameras to tour the Mesa Historical Museum complex in the dark. One of the museum's buildings that was explored was the auditorium of the former Lehi School, thought to be one of the most haunted locations on the property. Visitors and museum workers have reported seeing a spectral man, believed to be the spirit of the caretaker of the former school. According to Lisa Anderson, the common tale says he died of natural causes in the projector room of the auditorium sometime in the 1970s.

And if that isn't spooky enough for the average ghost hunter, guests stepped cautiously into the room where an interactive display from the once-popular local *Wallace and Ladmo* TV show offers childhood memories. Things become eerie when, suddenly, the theme song of the local children's program begins playing at will in the museum, usually when volunteers are working in the building alone. To play the song, the museum director noted, the music has to be physically selected, but this will happen when no one is in the room to do so. "Ho Ho, Ha Ha, Hee Hee, Ha Ha, Ho Ho, Ha Ha. Hee Hee. Ha Ha, Hooooooo!"

PEORIA HIGH SCHOOL
11200 NORTH EIGHTY-THIRD AVENUE
PEORIA, AZ 85345

Peoria High School was originally located in the back of a general store/post office and had a single teacher in 1919, but after a railroad was built through the city, a new building was opened in 1922, enrolling fifty students. At its opening, the school, built in the Spanish Colonial Revival style, was the largest structure in town and contained period luxuries, like indoor plumbing. In the next few decades, the school was the only Arizonan high school that continued to allow Japanese American students to attend during World War II. In 1962, it was the first in the area to allow Black students to participate in sports.

The main building, Old Main, was closed in 2008 for renovations, which began in 2012 and ended in 2014. The renovation added modernized classrooms, labs and other teaching spaces, as well as a student lounge. After its reopening, the building also housed the district's nontraditional high school, the Peoria Flex Academy. The district's Medicine, Engineering and Technology (MET) Academy shares the space with the center, though the school district acquired the Arizona Challenger Space Center building in 2017 with plans to move the academy into the space center. By 2019,

Peoria High School's Old Main was constructed in 1922. *Wikimedia.*

the district's board members had voted to repurpose the center into an arts center where students from any high school could take specialized art classes.

In 2019, Old Main was listed in the National Register of Historic Places.

Another high school auditorium that has made the list as one of the most haunted educational spaces in Arizona is the performing arts center in Peoria High School. According to one former theater teacher, the ghost that haunts the school is the spirit of a student who fell from the catwalk above the stage, although the school administrators are pretty vague when it comes to confirming or denying that particular rumor.

One former student noted, "It was the catwalk in the old theater, which is now used as a classroom. Weird things happen in the room—sudden chills, computers turning themselves on and hearing whispers in your ear."

An anonymous graduate added,

> *The female student who is rumored to have died in the former theater fell off the catwalk in the theater building, and no, the building was never remodeled—it has been the same for decades. There are several versions of how she fell—tripped, pushed—nobody knows. A lot of weird things*

happen during the day, but really weird things happen at night! Doors open and close, lights flicker, the faucets in the lobby bathrooms turn on and off by themselves. The ghost messes with the school performances, and the sound system has abruptly cut out during opening night, even though it worked perfectly fine during the earlier rehearsal. The catwalks stay locked during performances, and all light technicians stay in the sound booth. Some students have seen the girl in the dressing room bathrooms. We like to refer to the ghost as Rebecca, and whenever something odd happens, that is who the students blame and declare Rebecca is messing with us again.

Another graduate added, "I was a senior at Peoria during the 2006–7 school year. It was the weird happenings at Peoria High School that contributed my desires to become a paranormal investigator. I hope to conduct an investigation there some time in the future and hopefully put Rebecca to peace."

GEORGE WASHINGTON CARVER MUSEUM AND CULTURAL CENTER
415 EAST GRANT STREET
PHOENIX, AZ 85004

The George Washington Carver Museum and Cultural Center is housed in an early historic Phoenix high school building. When the school opened in 1926, it was known as Phoenix Union Colored High School. It was a segregated school for Black students in the Phoenix metropolitan area. The name of the school was changed to George Washington Carver High School in 1943.

The school was constructed on the grounds of a former four-acre landfill and was once heavily surrounded by small factories and warehouses. There were protests about the school's location, since it was so close to an industrial and contaminated area. Phoenix physicians feared the site was a "hot bed and nucleus of virulent contagious diseases" for the students and their families.

Carver High School began as the only educational option for Black students in the Phoenix area. The school turned out to be a first-rate educational institution due to the great quality and motivation of its teachers and staff. The students were inspired to always do their best. The school's population continued to grow. Carver was remodeled and enlarged in 1948, when

Above: George Washinton Carver School/Museum. *Wikimedia*.

Opposite: A statue of George Washington Carver. *Wikimedia*.

new shop facilities and a one-thousand-seat stadium were added. The students of Carver became inspiring scholars, athletes and artists.

In 1953, an Arizona court ruled school segregation to be unconstitutional. Carver's students were integrated into other existing Phoenix high schools. Carver closed its doors as a high school in 1954. The school's once-busy halls became cold and dreary storage areas for the Phoenix School District until 1991. The building was almost demolished, but a group of alumni joined together to save their alma mater.

The building and the almost five acres of land it sits on were honored and listed in the National Register of Historic Places in 1991. The parking lot and sports stadium remain silent, but the academic building is again filled with voices and laughter. These days, the offices and classrooms have been converted into various galleries. One room commemorates buffalo soldiers. Another room is filled with Carver Monarchs' athletic photographs, trophies and newspaper clippings.

Dee Roberts of the AzPrism paranormal team was fortunate to explore the old high school with her paranormal group. She reported that the most active area of the building was the second floor, where they encountered a shadow figure running in the hallway.

"We were set up to record an EVP session," Dee recalled. "Soon, we began to hear voices, like teens talking. Their voices were soft, almost a whisper, as though they were chatting without permission in a classroom. It was about that same time when we saw the shadow figure run down the hall—perhaps late for class!"

The current board president of the George Washington Carver Museum and Cultural Center noted that when the property was under construction in 1925, there was a caretaker house built on the site. It is assumed by the board members and volunteers that the spirit of the caretaker has stayed behind to watch over the property. The reports from the group state his presence has been felt in various areas on the old school grounds. Folks often report feeling watched by a protective gentleman, but when they look around, there is no one there.

PIONEER LIVING MUSEUM, OR THE GORDON SCHOOL
3907 WEST PIONEER ROAD
PHOENIX, AZ 85086

The Pioneer Living Museum is a collection of historic buildings that have been moved to one location from various points in Arizona so they can be restored and preserved for future generations to enjoy. The living museum is considered a "classroom without walls."

The Gordon School building is an original structure that once stood in Gordon Canyon, about thirty miles east of Payson, Arizona, on the Mogollon Rim. It was once the home of William Gordon and his family, and it was later transformed to a place of education when the family moved to Grapevine, Arizona. The schoolhouse was used from 1885 to 1930. Unfortunately, the original school records were misplaced and lost when Gila County split from Yavapai, so the exact year of the school's construction is unconfirmed.

The interior of the log cabin structure represents a typical 1890s territorial schoolhouse. All eight grade levels received their studies in the one-room

Gordon School building is located at the Pioneer Living Museum in Phoenix. *Wikimedia.*

schoolhouse. School was held between March and November to avoid the cold winter months.

The schoolhouse became the first completely restored historical building at the Pioneer Living Museum, and a dedication ceremony was held on October 23, 1966. The school and teacherage cabin are examples of the lengths to which the museum has gone to accurately restore historic buildings. Written on the blackboard is, "Faith, Foresight, and Fortitude Equal Pioneer Spirit."

The caretaker for the museum's twenty-six buildings dating from the nineteenth century to Arizona's statehood in 1912 never expected to hear children singing in the old schoolhouse when he took on his job, but these days, he hardly notices the activity.

Guests and staff have heard the voices of the schoolchildren talking and whispering "in class" and around the grounds of the Gordon School. Apparitions of the children have been seen seated in the wooden desks in the classroom and playing in the desert outside the log cabin school. The ghostly students are usually seen for just a few minutes before they dismiss themselves to recess.

GRACE COURT SCHOOL, OR THE ADAMS SCHOOL
830 WEST ADAMS STREET
PHOENIX, AZ 85007

The Adams School was built in 1911 by the John Roberts Company using a design created by architect Harrison Albright. At that time, the Adams School was tagged as the largest and most modern school in the city of Phoenix. In 1952, the name of the school was changed to Grace Court School to honor Grace Court, who served as the school's principal from 1918 to 1952. The school closed its doors to students in 1977 due to its structural deterioration and potential fire risk. It was reopened as an office building in 2005.

Around 2017, a woman by the name of Christy Jean was an employee of one of the offices in the Grace Court building. She had been working in the historic landmark for about one year. Everyone had witnessed doors slamming and swinging open, lights turning on and off and the telephone (which was not hooked up for service) ringing inside the elevator compartment.

Grace Court School, 1924. *Courtesy of Ryan Vander Ark.*

Grace Court School. *Author's collection.*

There was always an uneasy feeling about the second floor, as though someone was watching and you were not alone.

Christy shared a couple of ghostly experiences with me, the ones that made her a believer in the unknown and that perhaps Grace Court School was haunted. One morning, Christy arrived at work extra early, and it was still very dark outside. As she began to park her car, she looked up and noticed that some of the second-floor classroom lights were on. She observed a dark, shadowy figure of a man move past the window very quickly. The mysterious shadow appeared in the window a second time, only his reflection was caught in the mirrored glass of the building next door. Christy carefully exited her vehicle and flagged the night security guard to escort her into the building. After all, the workplace is located in the Phoenix downtown area, where the outlying streets are frequented by unpleasant folks. She was not about to enter the building alone. Christy and the security guard checked each floor of the building but found no one.

On a lighter note, Christy chuckled about another encounter she had with ghosts in the ladies' room. While she was in a stall, the toilet paper roll in the adjoining stall began to spin rapidly, causing toilet paper to rise in a heaping pile. She bent over slightly and glanced under the stall. She could see no feet! Thinking one of her coworkers was playing a joke on her, she left her stall and quickly opened the door to the adjacent stall. There was no one in sight! Christy quickly ran out of the restroom and was nervous to go back alone.

TREVOR G. BROWNE HIGH SCHOOL
7402 WEST CATALINA DRIVE
PHOENIX, AZ 85033

Trevor G. Browne High School (also known as Trevor Browne High School) is part of the Phoenix Union High School District in Phoenix, Arizona. The school began to accept students in the fall of 1972 and was named after Trevor Goff Browne, a Canadian-born man who taught at Harvard Medical School. Browne, who died in 1977, donated the land on which Trevor Browne High School was built.

When construction workers were building the auditorium in the early '90s, one of the workers fell off a high beam and was killed instantly on impact. They say you can hear moans and cries of pain in the auditorium at night.

A current theater instructor at Trevor Browne High School claims the story of the construction worker may simply be an urban legend. She was close friends with the former theater teacher who was employed at the school when it was built and found a few documents to confirm the story. She also heard tales of a girl who went missing around the time the theater was built. Students swear they have seen her wandering around the theater. Students were performing a show when they witnessed a big black blob floating over the set. The production crew noted that they saw a girl with black hair in the hallways. It turns out that the girl who went missing also had black hair! There may be a ghost, but it is not the spirit of a construction worker.

A Trevor Browne student noted, "I went to school there in 1981, and I was in the drama class. I was told by drama classmates the story of a young boy who had fallen off the catwalk and died. It is said that he could often be seen walking across the stage toward the end of a performance. I had the starring role as the main character in one of the plays presented on stage at the school. I saw his ghost during the last two nights of the performance of our play *The Elves and the Shoemaker*."

Elves can be quite mischievous, and apparently, the ghostly boy is quite the prankster, too!

FRANKLIN POLICE AND FIRE HIGH SCHOOL
1645 WEST McDOWELL ROAD
PHOENIX, AZ 85007

Franklin Police and Fire High School is a high school in the Phoenix Union High School District. Franklin's enrollment comprises over three hundred students and hosts ninth- through twelfth-graders. Phoenix Union's Franklin Police and Fire High School is the first of its kind in the nation, offering a high school education and a head start in a career in public safety. Public safety professionals teach the career classes, and the school partners with the City of Phoenix, its police and fire departments and other agencies to provide students with real-world opportunities, such as internships, physical training and special employment programs.

Franklin School was built in 1926 by the Phoenix Elementary School District. Wings were added to the building in 1935 and 1936, and the school was expanded to its current configuration in 1945. The school, designed by local architect Jay Knapp, has important decorative elements, including porthole gable ventilators, cast stone tablets and keystones and a frieze-like panel with an inscription of the school's name.

After Phoenix Elementary was closed, Phoenix Union used the building to house its Desiderata Program for Special Needs Students in the 1990s. The school fell into disrepair and stood abandoned for several years. Phoenix Union purchased it in 2004 and took on the task of bringing the old school building back to life, dealing with environmental issues with the property and strictly adhering to the building's historical restoration. The section of the building constructed in the 1920s and 1930s required hardwood flooring and custom wood windows and doors. The replacement tiles on the roof were fabricated locally to the color and size specifications of the period.

Maintenance workers, students and school principals have all reported ghostly encounters in the building. One teen had an experience with a presence in the men's bathroom during one Halloween season. The student said he entered the restroom/shower room at the school and noted that the stall door was shut. He assumed someone was using the commode. He stood patiently at the sink, grooming himself and combing his hair. Finally, the toilet flushed, and the teen waited for about a minute for the person in the stall to leave. But no one emerged from behind the secured door. Puzzled, the lad decided to peek inside and found the stall empty. He quickly ran out of the lavatory and refused to enter that restroom alone again.

Ghost stories began to circulate throughout the school and made their way to the principal's office. At first, the principal brushed off the alleged ghost stories as high school gossip and eventually said, "If there was a ghost, it was playful, harmless and helpful."

Even the custodial staff was spooked by the unexplained haunting. The custodians shared an office in the school basement that was equipped with security cameras, desks and cleaning supplies. They claimed they heard footsteps on the west side of the building after school hours. The security camera system showed no interference. Many of the unexplained incidents happened in the west wing near the science lab.

One of the custodians recalled a morning when he was carrying a case of water bottles and wished that someone was nearby and could open the door

Franklin School. *Wikimedia.*

for him. Suddenly, the door opened. He assumed his partner had unlocked it for him, and he stepped inside. Surprisingly, the room was completely empty. Then the door slowly closed behind him. He was puzzled. That heavy door was always locked.

Once, a supply of new classroom wall clocks was delivered to the school. One of the custodians set the time on each clock and carefully hung them on the walls on a Friday afternoon. By Monday, "the clocks in the west building had been moved back in time by one hour." She ran to the principal's office shouting, "The ghost moved the clocks' time back!"

After some time, the custodians and the ghost made peace. The custodians even began calling the ghost by the name Frank. They learned to accept the friendly spirit and were no longer afraid of his antics. A curious employee tried to find out who Frank might be. The only clue she could find was a story shared by her father, who had been a student at Franklin School in the 1940s. He informed his daughter the name given to the ghost back then was George.

One theory proclaimed the ghost was a deceased worker who had fed coal to the large furnace in the basement during the chilly winter months. Boldly, the custodians learned a valuable lesson in paranormal theory. "Never be afraid of the dead—be more afraid of the living!"

MARCOS DE NIZA HIGH SCHOOL
6000 SOUTH LAKESHORE DRIVE
TEMPE, AZ 85283

Marcos De Niza High School was established in 1971 and is a popular four-year high school located in the southern neighborhood of Tempe, Arizona. The school is known for its "outstanding curriculum, comprehensive fine arts and athletic programs, and a wide variety of extracurricular activities." It is also known for a few ghostly specters.

DarkHaunts.com reports that the school's ghost has nothing to do with a student or teacher of Marcos De Niza but reflects the tale of an unfortunate construction worker who died in the building process of the auditorium in 1970.

Former students report that a man fell during the construction of the drama room. They say his presence has been felt and seen walking along the catwalk during school plays and performances. The drama room also doubles as the music room. Band and orchestra members often find their instruments have been misplaced or moved about the room.

The ghost is often detected after 9:00 p.m. trying to finish the construction work he initiated so many years before. People are leery of staying in the auditorium alone after 9:00 p.m. Some students have reported hearing voices when no one else is there or feeling someone touch them on the shoulder. Others have witnessed a shadowy figure in the auditorium. The students and staff have nicknamed the playful ghost Paco.

The drama and theater department at Marcos De Niza High School is one of the best in the valley area. If you plan to attend a performance, check the seat next to you. You might have someone unseen watching the show by your side!

Remember, a common tale among other high schools in Phoenix say that a construction worker fell and died after hitting their stage. It is not known where this disastrous tale began, but the claims are many. There is no doubt the energies of many construction workers remain behind. They are often proud of the quality of their craftsmanship and continue to showcase their talented work.

A former student of Marcos De Niza High claimed they had a personal experience with the ghostly construction worker, Paco. It was an ordinary school day until the performing arts students arrived to do the annual Paco Tour in the auditorium. As one of the guests on the tour, this new student

Marcos de Niza High School in Tempe. *Author's collection.*

wasn't expecting much. The staff and upperclassmen began to scare up some stories to frighten the gullible freshmen. Some of the students started to get very nervous as they headed up the winding stairs that led up to the dark, ominous catwalk. Some say Paco's footsteps can be heard up there, trailing behind you. But if you turn to look, no one will be there!

It was the nervous freshman's turn to climb the ladder that leads to the catwalk. As she hung on to each rung, the atmosphere seemed to get colder and colder. Being a skeptic, she was reluctant to blame it on Paco. She carefully followed her friend, who was terrified of ghosts, and began to feel a strange electricity in the air. She blew it off as a breeze in a higher elevation and continued to walk on. The feeling just never went away. Her friend noticed the same chill in the air and turned to whisper, "I know you are thinking I am paranoid, but I feel something in the air and it's not normal."

The girl walked about ten or twelve feet when her friend yelped and literally grabbed on to another girl directly in front of her. In a split second, the student swore she could feel a breeze blow directly in front of them. It came from the left, swept to the right and then disappeared. The girl's friend's eyes were as wide as saucers, and she announced that she had felt something touch her back. The upper-class students around them found the situation amusing and started to laugh. A boy who was standing behind them remained silent. His eyes were wide as well, and his face seemed pale. The girls knew the boy had seen or felt something, too, but he refused to admit it.

To this day, the girls are not sure whether it was Paco checking out the school's new arrivals. Nevertheless, it was a very strange scene.

A.J. MATTHEWS CENTER, ARIZONA STATE UNIVERSITY
950 CADY MALL
TEMPE, AZ 85281

Originally the first library on campus, the A.J. Matthews Center continues to represent the spirit of learning and creativity at ASU. The School of Human Evolution and Social Change maintains archaeological and physical anthropology collections, meeting spaces and student and faculty offices here. Student Media, where students publish the *State Press*, the campus's daily newspaper and the seventh-largest publication in Arizona, is located in the A.J. Matthews Center. Comprehensive support services for students with disabilities, including alternative print formats and interpretation, are provided by Disability Resources, located in the A.J. Matthews Center.

The building was constructed in 1930 and was named for Arthur John Matthews, the first in ASU history to serve with the title "president." Matthews held this title from the early 1900s to 1930.

In October 2002, the MVD Ghostchasers were invited by staff to investigate the hauntings of the Matthews Center. Their mission was to search for spirits and investigate the stories that have puzzled ASU for many years, including the narrow back staircases and tunnels that can be accessed from the basement. Some of the paranormal team members felt uneasy on the fifth-floor landing of the back staircase. They said they smelled the faint odor of smoke and felt a burning sensation in their throats. A light was switched back on after being set in the off position. They felt as if someone was watching them when they stood on the rooftop to catch the full moon and view the campus.

ASU's Matthews Center. *Wikimedia.*

They were told the Matthews Center was once the university's main library and that the *Hayden's Ferry Review* office downstairs was used as an autopsy room when the building was home to nursing students.

The staff told the MVD Ghostchasers the undocumented legend of a librarian who perished in a fire when she was trapped on the back stairways of the Matthews Center. Some workers and students have reported seeing a woman wandering the stairs, searching for an exit.

The group was also told that the anthropology department kept Native bones in the building. The U.S. Military was said to have given ASU Native bones to study, after which people started seeing the ghosts of Apache warriors wandering the halls late at night. Once the bones were returned to their appropriate tribes, the activity ceases. An anthropology processor stepped up to note that the only bones worth mentioning belonged to the bodies of two gorillas, not Natives, as rumored.

A gorilla was flown into the Phoenix Zoo via Hugh Heffner's private plan to serve as a companion for Phoenix's famous gorilla Hazel. Jack died of valley fever soon after his arrival, and his bones were donated to the ASU anthropology department. The professor said he had never seen the ghost of the gorilla but may have heard his haunting primate holler late at night!

Many students and staff have heard variations of the tale of the ghostly librarian. Some heard she died in a fire in the building. Some heard she died off campus in a horrific car accident, and still others claim she died by suicide. No matter what her cause of death was, many have seen a female figure wandering through the hallways. No record has been found to document the death, but almost everyone has heard the story or knows someone who has claimed to have seen the ghostly apparition. One employee who worked in the basement of Matthews Center beginning in 1979 claimed she heard the librarian along with a fireman who tried to rescue her on a back staircase.

The MVD Ghostchasers told the staff, "She didn't have to die here in order to make her presence known here. Perhaps she comes back to the center because she loved her job, and it was a location she really liked."

The crew who worked in the basement area reported hearing sounds coming from the other side of a door that led out to the massive underground tunnels that wind between the buildings on campus. A small group of the paranormal investigators entered the dark area with flashlights and wandered through the never-ending tunnel system. After determining the noises came from water and electrical and cable lines, the team returned and assured the workers they had nothing to fear. It was sure great to explore those catacombs!

VIRGINIA G. PIPER CENTER FOR CREATIVE WRITING, ARIZONA STATE UNIVERSITY
450 EAST TYLER MALL
TEMPE, AZ 85281

Originally built in 1907, the Virginia G. Piper Writers House once served as the home of ASU presidents. Arthur John Matthews (1904–30), Ralph W. Swetman (1930–33) and Grady Gammage (1933–59) resided in the historic president's cottage until it became the Alumni House and Alumni Executive Office (1961–72). Most recently, it was home to the University Archives (1972–95). In 2005, the building once again saw more renovations, including gardens and a back patio addition. It is now used as the Virginia G. Piper

Center for Creative Writing, which offers offices for staff, creative writing classrooms and a gathering space for readings, receptions and events.

Along with the impressive University Club and Old Main, the Piper Writers House is one of the last remaining historic buildings on the ASU-Tempe campus. The house is one of the last remaining buildings designed by the popular territorial architect James Creighton, who also designed the original ASU Normal School (now demolished).

The President's House was a symmetrical two-story Western Colonial brick building with a copper shingle roof. The central entry was originally a projecting hipped porch with classical detailing. The porch was enclosed in 1937 with four-light casement windows and a twelve-light entry door with eight-pane sidelights. The main house had a two-story bay window on its west side and a two-story bay with a fireplace on its east side. The roof was hipped with projecting gables and featured boxed eaves and a central hipped dormer. In 1931, two rooms and a bathroom were added to the northwest corner of the house.

There is a rumor that the home is often visited by the ghost of Dixie Gammage, the wife of ASU president Grady Gammage, as well as Grady

Virginia G. Piper Center, ASU. *Wikimedia.*

Gammage himself, who died in an upstairs bedroom in December 1959. The popular couple met in Prescott, Arkansas, and fell in love. Due to a ten-year age gap, the couple decided it was best to marry in Prescott, Arkansas, in 1913. They relocated to Tucson, Arizona, where Mr. Gammage attended the university.

After graduation, Dr. and Mrs. Gammage went to Winslow, where he became the superintendent of Winslow schools. From Winslow, the couple moved to Flagstaff in 1925, following Dr. Gammage's appointment to the presidency of the Arizona State College there. The Gammage family was living in Tempe when Dr. Gammage became the president of Arizona State University.

Known for her civic and social activities, Dixie Gammage was a past president of the Tempe Woman's Club and a member of the Tempe Methodist Church. She was active in community affairs until ill health forced her to give up many of her duties.

She became an invalid and was confined to the second floor of the house, where she spent many of her last days. She traveled to Paradise Valley Sanatorium near San Diego, California, in August 1948. She was sixty-four years old and had been under treatment for a heart and liver ailment. She passed away at the sanatorium on September 11 that year. After her death, she was purportedly seen on occasion walking past the second-story windows of the president's house, dressed in a bathrobe and wearing a hat.

A gentleman who was the former university archivist at the ASU Library often reported witnessing ghostly happenings at both the Matthews Center and the Virginia G. Piper Center. He claimed he had a paranormal experience in the Piper Writers House when it was used as the archives building between the 1980s and the 1990s. His office was located across the hall from the southwestern corner bedroom where President Grady Gammage died. He remembered hearing a creaky door close downstairs while he was working upstairs late at night. He went down the stairs looking for a possible explanation but did not find the cause—or an intruder!

Grady Gammage was born in Arkansas in August 1892. He died of a heart attack the morning of December 22, 1959, as his physician was examining him. He had complained he was very tired and wasn't feeling well the night before. His death came unexpectedly; he was sixty-seven years old. He was honored and remained in state beneath the rotunda at the Arizona State Capital. He was buried in Greenwood Cemetery in Phoenix.

Another university spokesperson noted that he has heard stories of ghostly apparitions being seen in the building, along with lights turning on late at

Old Main, ASU, 1910. *Wikimedia*.

night. In the 1990s, a group of students known as the Devils Advocates gave tours to prospective students, new enrollees and their parents throughout the year. The volunteer guides told stories of the school's past, sometimes adding a little folklore to the tales. They, too, believe the president's home is haunted and jokingly relay a rumor that Mrs. Gammage used to sunbathe in the nude on the roof!

VULTURE CITY SCHOOL
36610 355TH AVENUE
WICKENBURG, AZ 85390

In 1863, Henry Wickenburg discovered gold. Legend has it, the name Vulture came to him after he shot a rather large vulture with his rifle and then spotted shining nuggets of gold while prodding the fallen inedible bird with his boot. The Vulture Mine went on to become one of Arizona's richest gold mines and sparked the development of Arizona Territory and the city of Phoenix. In the 1880s and 1890s, Vulture City's population grew to almost five thousand and featured a large stone assay office, miners' dormitories, houses for company officials, a mess hall, a school, a post office and an

Vulture City School. *Courtesy of Dee Roberts and Debe Branning.*

eighty-stamp mill. It is estimated that the Vulture Mine produced more than $200 million worth of gold and silver. The exact amount is unknown due to theft, or high grading, for which several men were murdered or hanged. President Roosevelt's executive order in 1942 ended the mining activity. In time, the town fell into disarray and became a living ghost town.

Above: Vulture City School grounds. *Author's collection.*

Left: Vulture City School's playground slide. *Author's collection.*

Electricity came to the Vulture Mine in the early 1900s. Miners and a few families began to settle and build small cabins in Vulture City. A schoolhouse with two schoolmarms operated there from 1908 to 1915 as the overall population seemed to stabilize around five hundred. The small school educated the children of around three hundred mining families.

Eventually, over forty cabins housed these families, and Vulture City became a self-contained small town. Records estimate the population of the mining town ranged from five hundred to five thousand residents. At Vulture City's peak, it was reported to be the largest community in Arizona. Some three thousand townsfolk were said to have lived in the town in the 1930s, when a second schoolhouse was built to educate the additional children.

The county superintendent often paid a visit to the rough-and-tumble mining town schools to be assured the children were receiving a good education and a promising future. During his inspection in October 1910, the superintendent found an excellent schoolhouse. He observed a well-appointed building and a classroom of twenty-seven pupils under the direction of Meta Dickinson. He noted everything was going along splendidly and believed the camp would have a fine class throughout the year. A more generous hand than the one the company showed toward the local children had never been shown in the county. Meta Dickinson seemed to be strong in her work, which was a great relief for the superintendent.

The MVD Ghostchasers were fortunate to hold a Vulture Mine Paranormal Camp on the grounds of the old mining town in January 2001. Guests were invited to set up sleeping accommodations, such as tents, small camping trailers and RVs in the parking area near the old historic schoolhouses. The paranormal explorers hiked along the trails of the old mine and investigated the assay house, ball plant, generator building, bunkhouse, brothel, glory hole, Verde Flat Cemetery and, of course, the schoolhouses. In the late 1990s and early 2000s, the site was still a bit raw, but the activity was always fresh and the spirits were quite welcoming to the groups who attended the ghost hunt.

Around sunset, a few members of the group passed by the deserted playground on their way back to the camping facilities. A forgotten teeter-totter and rusty swing set still graced the abandoned schoolhouse grounds.

Debe Branning noted, "While I explored the area, I noted the air was very still. There was no wind, not even a breeze. I stopped in my tracks in the middle of the pathway when I suddenly noticed one of the swings was slowly moving back and forth just a few inches. I grabbed my camera and began taking a few photographs. The momentum of the old wooden swing

began to pick up, and soon, it was soaring back and forth, higher and higher. The swing next to it remained perfectly still."

Later that evening, a group made themselves cozy in the newer schoolhouse building. All three of the investigators confirmed they heard a few notes playing on the weathered upright piano with a broken keyboard. Years later, in 2010, Travel Channel's *Ghost Adventures* witnessed the same phenomena and declared the old school building was one of the most active buildings on the grounds.

Dee Roberts of AzPrism Paranormal had her own paranormal encounter in the haunted school in Vulture City.

I was investigating one evening at the old schoolhouse. My team had a lot of paranormal activity throughout our time spent there. Earlier in the evening, I had witnessed the swing attached to the school yard swing set at the rear of the schoolyard start to move back and forth. I also heard children's laughter. Christy and I wandered back into the schoolhouse. I was standing up against the wall space between two windows. We started an EVP session, asking if anyone was in the room with us. Still leaning at the wall, I added, "If you are here, let us know by doing something." The next thing I knew, my back was shoved from the wall by a pair of unseen

Opposite: Vulture City School's playground swings. *Author's collection.*

Above: Vulture City School's piano. *Author's collection.*

Vulture City School's playground teeter-totter. *Author's collection.*

hands and flung into Christy. The force was so hard that it flung me about eight feet. If Christy had not caught me, I would have been laid out on the floor. After that happened, the activity level in the schoolhouse calmed down.

Other paranormal teams who have investigated the schools have heard footsteps, banging on the walls, children speaking, boys chuckling and young girls crying. Others have witnessed shadow figures standing in the doorway on moonlit nights.

Nearby is the old Vulture City Cemetery (Verde Flat Cemetery), the final resting spot for many Hispanic families and children who died in birth. There are several miners and their wives, along with their young schoolchildren, who did not survive the epidemics or infectious diseases of the era, including the influenza pandemic of 1918, who were buried there. These graves are marked by simple white crosses. Their lives cut short, many of the miners' children still play near their familiar house of learning.

Do the spirits remain in Vulture City to protect the mine's riches? See for yourself! Vulture City is open most weekends and welcomes both historians and ghost hunters alike.

5
MOHAVE COUNTY

HACKBERRY ELEMENTARY SCHOOL
OFF ROUTE 66
HACKBERRY, AZ 70645

One of the most visited towns along the western end of Route 66 in Arizona is Hackberry. The settlement was originally a mining camp at the foot of the Peacock Mountains. Ranching and mining brought the railroad to Hackberry in 1882, and it transported local cattle and carried ore gathered from the Hackberry Silver Mine. When the mine closed, close to $3 million worth of gold and silver had been excavated. Hackberry's temporary prosperity is showcased in its now-abandoned elementary school.

Most of the schools in the era were wooden shacks, barns or borrowed churches, but the community of Hackberry came together and commissioned a grand, almost castle-like stone building. In May 1917, the school's board of trustees called for bids for the erection of "a one-story public-school building, to accommodate at least 80 pupils and cost not to exceed Seven Thousand Dollars; building to include all necessary wardrobe closest, teacher's room, library room, etc., and to have chimney and fresh air vents for heating and ventilating purposes and to be as nearly fire-proof as the sum to be expended will permit."

The winning design was an ornate Mission-style building with red roof tiles, two tiny decorative towers and a Spanish-style bell. The board of

The historic Hackberry Schoolhouse, 1927. *Courtesy of Chance Houston.*

trustees hired Axel Ericson to oversee the task, and he completed the work in August 1917.

The school had two classrooms, two bathrooms, a kitchen and living quarters for a teacher. Children attended Hackberry Elementary School from kindergarten to the eighth grade. But by 1994, the board of trustees had decided the little school should be closed.

Today, children are bussed to schools several miles away, leaving Hackberry, along with its school, looking more and more like a ghost town. Hackberry Elementary School is privately owned, locked up and fenced off. Former students still have memories of riding their horses to school, ringing the school bell, raising and lowering the flag and running from yellow jackets.

Hackberry Elementary School was much more than an elementary school; it was also a local gathering place. It was a building grand enough for celebrations yet dignified enough for any solemn occasion, including funerals.

On August 27, 1918, seventeen-year-old Henry Bacon Jr. (the son of a Hackberry cattle rancher) met death under peculiar circumstances in a reservoir nine miles south of the town. Bacon and two of his companions had been riding in the vicinity of the reservoir when one of the boys proposed they go for a swim. Henry's other friend dissented because the water was very cold but agreed to show them how to swim their horses across the deep part of the pond.

The reservoir sloped down from a few inches in depth at the upper end to about fourteen feet deep close to the dam. The young men forced their horses into the water, and after disporting for some time, they again proposed to go swimming. Two of the young men went in and kept close to the embankment as they went across the deep part of the pond. One of them made it across safely, but when that boy looked back, he saw Henry Bacon slowly sinking. He called out to the third boy, and they dove back into the water to try to save the drowning boy. The other boys reached Bacon just as he was sinking for the third time. Bacon grasped onto them, and they struggled to swim to the water's edge. The boys finally got Bacon to paddle along a few feet, but finally, the young man gave up and sank. One of the young men dove down to retrieve him while the other hurried off to secure a rope. Henry Bacon slipped from this grip again, and if the attempted rescuer had not been dragged to shore, he would have slipped under the water and downed as well. The young men made every effort to locate and rescue Henry Bacon, but all their efforts were to no avail, and they sent word to Hackberry.

A group of men returned in a vehicle, and they continued the rescue efforts. The water was cold, which impeded the men's work, but Henry's body was located and brought to the surface later that afternoon. It was a sad group who arrived back in Hackberry that afternoon. Henry Bacon Jr. was one of the most popular young men in the area, and his untimely death put a pall over the entire town. He had been his father's superintendent on the range.

His funeral was held at Hackberry Elementary School on Thursday afternoon. Over one hundred people arrived from Kingman, and hundreds came from the surrounding countryside to pay their last sad duty to a most estimable boy. Flowers covered the bier, and the large schoolroom overflowed with blooms and greenery.

A line of automobiles reached almost the entire distance between the schoolhouse and the little graveyard on the hill, and many people followed on foot. The death of Henry Bacon was another sad event experienced by this admired family. During the preceding few years, the family had lost eight children and their mother. The only ones left to mourn were Henry's father, one brother, four sisters and various relatives.

LEE WILLIAMS HIGH SCHOOL, OR WHITE CLIFF MIDDLE SCHOOL
400 GRANDVIEW AVENUE
KINGMAN, AZ 86401

Lee Williams High School was the second comprehensive high school in the town of Kingman, Arizona. It opened on August 9, 2012, a year later than originally planned. It is named for Richard Lee Williams, a former school principal and firefighter who died while fighting in the Doxol disaster in 1973. The Doxol disaster was the result of a boiling liquid expanding vapor explosion that occurred during a propane transfer from a Doxol railroad car to a storage tank on the Getz rail siding near Andy Devine Avenue/Route 66. The school's mascot is the Volunteer.

In 1917, Mohave County Union High School was opened at this site. It later became known as Kingman High School. In 1993, a new Kingman High School–North campus was opened for sophomores, juniors and seniors. Freshmen attended the old (South) school. As the population of Kingman continued to grow, Kingman North became the permanent high school. Kingman South was renamed White Cliff Middle School.

The football stadium at White Cliff Middle School in Kingman, Arizona, gives an entirely different meaning to the term *team spirit*. This football field was built on what was once the Pioneer Cemetery of Kingman. The Pioneer Cemetery was known as the original cemetery in Kingman from 1900 to 1917.

Around 1903, Jennie Bauters, Jerome's most famous and loved madam, left Jerome, Arizona, and headed for a new boom town called Acme (now known as Goldfield). Jennie's gambling suitor Clement C. Leigh followed her there. After a time, Jennie began to feel he was becoming somewhat of a threat. In September 1905, Leigh needed money to settle a bad debt. With anger in his heart and a gun in his hand, Leigh bounded over to Jennie's place and demanded she hand over all her cash. An argument ensued, and Jennie tried to flee the building. Leigh chased after her, firing several shots at the frightened woman. One bullet struck and wounded her as she ran frantically into the street. Leigh approached the paralyzed woman and fired a fatal shot to her head. He then pointed the gun at his chest and fired again. He lay down beside Jennie, ready to die. Instead, Leigh survived his suicide attempt and was carted off to jail. Jennie was mourned by all who loved her and was laid to rest in the Pioneer Cemetery in Kingman. In 1907, justice was served, and Leigh was hanged to death. He, too, was buried in the Kingman Pioneer Cemetery.

Lee Williams High School in Kingman. *Pinterest.*

Sometime around 1917, the county began the task of moving the graves of the dearly departed in Pioneer Cemetery to the new Mountain View Cemetery. Mohave County would not pay for these loved ones to be moved to the new location; it was the family's responsibility. So, some of the not so dearly departed, whose relatives either could not or would not come forward, were not moved. They were left behind at the deserted cemetery.

In 1944, before the cemetery's land was about to be repurposed, the owners offered to try to relocate the existing burial plots and bodies to a newer cemetery. Sadly, the county was charging $45 per plot for removal, which, in 1944, was equivalent to $600 today. Many families could not afford these prices, and as a result, many of the bodies remained unclaimed.

Mohave County donated the old Pioneer Cemetery property to the school board for the construction of a new high school. A stadium and parking lot replaced the hallowed grounds. They say that, in the 1940s, some youngsters who were playing on the football field began unearthing bones that were never moved to Mountain View Cemetery. Many local organizations were alarmed. Workmen discovered eleven burial sites and seven coffins. They also found artifacts such as medallions and pieces of jewelry. The contractor went so far as to contact a local tribe for a blessing of the land. The chief blessed those who stumbled on the grave sites and warned them that disturbed spirits could manifest and follow them. They immediately took action and had the remaining bodies exhumed and placed in a solitary grave on the property. There is a plaque dedicated to the unknown buried pioneers on the school's grounds.

Over the years, there have been reports of hauntings at the school. Many theorize the displaced souls were unhappy with their final resting spots being disrupted and paved over. Some say the ghosts began appearing at school events and the surrounding area, often wearing pioneer clothing or western wear.

Others noted they have felt unexplained cold spots throughout the school building. Students and teachers note there are certain areas in the building where they feel uneasy, and they say they try to avoid those locations. One such spot is an odd, narrow passageway that has a small, half-size door. They say it leads into a dark, windowless chamber that resembles a vault or tomb. It is not used today, and nobody seems to know what the chamber was once used for, but the tiny room was included in the building plans.

School staff members have noted that several spirits insist on remaining after school. They have heard footsteps in the hallways and have felt the eerie sensation of being followed or that they are not alone. They have heard knocking on the walls and doors and have seen lights flicker on and off. It's enough to make any brave soul a little cautious. Some have heard faint voices, children's laughter and an occasional disembodied voice demanding they "go home!"

Some of the staff have even reported seeing a little girl who appears and urges them to play a game of ball with her. Students and staff insist they have seen a man in a bowler hat and long black coat loitering around the school.

And as fate would have it, Jennie Bauters and her murderer, Clement Leigh, are now buried in the same grave and entombed forever in the endzone of a football field. So, if you are ever attending a big football game at the old stadium and the excitement begins to magnify, beware. The rising spirits might be from something other than the cheering crowd.

6

PIMA COUNTY

CATALINA HIGH SCHOOL: DISNEYLAND OF GHOSTS
3645 EAST PIMA STREET
TUCSON, AZ 85716

Catalina High School (also known as Catalina Magnet High School) is located on the north side of Tucson, Arizona, and serves approximately eight hundred students between the eighth and twelfth grades. Its name originates from the Santa Catalina Mountains north of Tucson. The school's mascot is the Trojan, and the school colors are royal blue and white.

In 1953, Tucson had only one high school, Tucson High, so the school board began discussing the construction of a second high school in the district to meet the area's population growth. In January 1957, the partially completed campus enrolled a full student body. There were many innovations to the school built for two thousand students. The new school contained a library, seventy-nine classrooms, two gyms, three conference rooms, a reference room, a cafeteria, a band room, an auto body shop, a bookstore and an auditorium. In some locations, ramps were installed instead of stairs. All the lockers in the school and gym were ventilated. The gymnasium could accommodate four thousand spectators and was the largest gymnasium in Arizona. Built as a state-of-the-art school, Catalina High presently has sixty-five regular classrooms and an eight-classroom science wing. R.T. Gridley was the first principal of Catalina High, and the first graduating class left the school in May 1957. Catalina's students voted for its first student council and student officers in September 1955 while they were still enrolled at Tucson High.

It was not until 1959 that the original plans for the school were completed. In the 1960s, Catalina High School was known as a Disneyland. Its architecture was viewed as lavishly modern and expensive, aimed at the higher-income students who attended Catalina from central Tucson and the Catalina Foothills. Shortly following the establishment of Catalina, many other high schools opened in the more affluent suburbs of Tucson. Students liked the Disneyland moniker so much that the Disneyland musical theme "Mickey Mouse" became the unofficial school song.

Reports of a ghostly janitor have been circulating since the early 1980s, when a group of Catalina High School janitors gathered together to discuss their encounters with the spirit of Martin Valencia.

The ghostly presence is not signaled by heavy bootsteps, howling winds or bangs on the wall; rather, it makes itself known using the squeaking and grating sounds of the caster wheels of a garbage can being pushed along the corridors of the high school.

It has been said that one janitor felt so tormented by the ghostly noises that he bolted from his locker to the nearest exit once his shift ended and the building lights were turned off. There have been both skeptics and believers among the custodial staff. Some custodians believe the spirit is the ghost of a dearly departed colleague who ended his afterhours shift in the late 1960s. Other coworkers laugh and suggest the idea of a haunting is absurd.

One janitor, who boasted he is only afraid of living people, admits he saw something when he was checking the restrooms on the night before graduation ceremonies in June 1980. He claims it was about 12:30 a.m., and he and his fellow custodians were working overtime to get ready for the upcoming ceremony. He heard the casters on the garbage can and began to look around the area. The hallway was lighted for about twenty-five feet. He saw a man in gray work clothes. The man was pushing a garbage can and walking away into the half-lighted hall. The janitor glanced again, and the man in gray was gone! At first, he thought the figure was one of his other coworkers, but when he returned to the auditorium, all the other custodians were there and accounted for, setting up chairs for the graduation ceremony.

A few months later, another janitor was stocking soap in the dispenser in the faculty lounge restroom at the end of the night shift. Instead of the squeaky casters, this workman heard footsteps coming up a ramp toward him. He slowly looked around but did not see anybody. Frozen in place, he stood quietly and began hearing the footsteps again! He was sure someone was in the building, so he waited—but nobody came. He finally gave up and decided to step outside to get some fresh air. There, he found the entire night crew waiting for him so they could lock the doors for the night and go home.

Other custodians have noted witnessing strange occurrences, such as doors slamming and trash bins going missing, along with cleaning supplies and utensils. The cleaning crew has a feeling the ghost is the spirit of a former employee, Martin Valencia, who died of a heart attack in the late 1960s while working in the high school building.

One of the custodians stated he knew Valencia and said he was a dedicated and conscious workman. The kitchen and home economics department was Valencia's favorite domain. The kitchen staff would set out a batch of cookies in the cafeteria for the night crew. Sometimes, the guys would take other treats. Martin would yell at them and scold them about that. Does Valencia's ghost return to protect the kitchen?

Some of the janitors believe the ghost stories are merely folklore or perhaps someone's mind playing tricks on them. It is eerie around Catalina High School at night. The old building creaks, and its maze of hallways gleam in the half light. It's the perfect environment for a ghost. But only the custodians are around when the spirit decides to appear.

TUCSON HIGH SCHOOL
400 NORTH SECOND AVENUE
TUCSON, AZ 85705

Tucson High School (now known as Tucson High Magnet School) is the oldest operating public high school in Arizona. On April 10, 1906, the Arizona Board of Regents determined that as of September 1, 1906, students from Arizona cities with a population of more than five thousand must complete the ninth grade before they are allowed to enroll in the University of Arizona's Preparatory Department.

The first day of class in the newly established Tucson High School occurred on September 10, 1906, with forty-five students who had started their education at the Plaza School at Thirteenth Street and Fourth Avenue.

Tucson Senior High School, Tucson, Arizona   68429   322

Tucson Senior High School postcard. *Wikimedia.*

After a few weeks, the high school students were relocated to a two-room building at 1010 East Tenth Street, the current location of Tucson Unified School District headquarters.

In 1908, they were moved to the newly constructed Tucson High School building at 501 East Sixth Street, which is currently Roskruge Elementary and Bilingual Magnet Middle School. Students remained at that location until they completed their high school years. By 1910, only ten students from that original class remained students.

The construction of Tucson High School's current main building began in 1923 and was completed in 1924, just in time for fall classes. Tucson High's main building was designed by Henry Jaastad and cost $750,000. The grand building, with its ornate details, such as Corinthian columns, stood as an architectural masterpiece then and remains so today. A magnificent icon, the main building, with its fourteen towering columns, welcomed classes ranging in size from 175 students in 1924 to over 3,500 students in 2016 (its largest class).

The 1987 film *Can't Buy Me Love*, starring Patrick Dempsey and Amanda Peterson, was filmed on location at the school when it was known as Tucson High School.

Graduates speak about a legendary tale of a male student who died by suicide in one of the classrooms in the vocational building on the high school's campus. It's reported that unexplained loud bangs, like feet hitting the floor, have been heard by teachers and students. Loud footsteps and chilling temperature drops have also been experienced at the school.

UNIVERSITY OF ARIZONA
TUCSON

OLD MAIN'S GHOST
1200 EAST UNIVERSITY BOULEVARD
TUCSON, AZ 85719

Old Main was constructed on the campus of the original Territorial University of Arizona College of Mines. It is located on the site of an ancient Native village that dates back well over ten thousand years. Carlos Maldenado was one of the workmen who supervised the construction of the building. He resided in Tucson from 1841 until his death in 1888. Some people believe his spirit lives on in the walls of Old Main.

Maldenado had a special interest in the university's first structure. He was known to have stayed in the unfinished building overnight on several occasions. He spent his evenings chatting with local Natives who stopped by to observe the creation of the grand facility "way out in the desert so far from town."

Maldenado felt it was important to stay close and keep an eye on the progress of the building, especially before the doors and windows were put in place. Some Tucson officials and residents were not happy the city had lost its bid to be the territorial capital city. They were doubly upset they had lost their opportunity to boast their rights to the Arizona Asylum for the Insane, which also ended up in Phoenix. Threats of vandalism were frequently spoken.

The saloons in Tucson were full of rumors of men secretly talking about burning the university building to the ground in an act of revenge. Then one morning, as the construction workers arrived to work on their horses and wagons, they noticed that Carlos Maldenado's wagon was securely tied to the hitching post outside the building. Assuming Maldenado was already

University of Arizona's Old Main. *Wikimedia.*

on the job, they yelled out his name, but all was silent. The workmen found the first floor empty, so they headed up to the unfinished second floor, where they encountered a strange morning breeze filtering through the structure.

Since Maldenado was known as a prankster by his friends all over town, the work crew began to think they were part of a practical joke. They found Maldenado sitting quietly in a wooden chair with his back to the workmen. Still thinking it was all a prank, the men snuck up behind their boss and tried to talk to him. But there was no answer or any movement.

The curious employees walked around the chair and discovered a very large buffalo skinner's knife deep in Carlos Maldenado's throat. Crimson-red blood saturated the dead man's clothing. The townspeople believed Carlos had attempted to scare off a group of angry men who had come to burn the unfinished building to the ground. The murder remains unsolved.

In 1938, years after the death of Carlos Maldenado, the Old Main building was neglected and declared unsafe by Tucson officials. After the Japanese attack on Pearl Harbor, Hawaii, in 1941, the Old Main building was used for training military officers. Remodeling was funded by the United States War Department.

Soon after the renovations began, workmen reported seeing the head and shoulders of a Mexican man floating in the air in the various rooms that were being worked on. Even though the rooms were dark due to the electrical system being torn out, ready for replacement, the workers

101

were able to see the phantom figure and identified the spirit of Carlos Maldenado from a photograph of the man that was taken during a social event in 1883.

A university regent and a female office clerk witnessed the ghostly apparition standing in a doorway. They reported the ghost looked straight at both of them and quickly vanished. Students, faculty and office personnel regularly see the shadowy form of a man at Old Main. He doesn't stay long enough to be photographed, but his presence continues to be felt—especially when renovations are active. Seems that Carlos Maldenado is still protecting Old Main from harm and danger.

HIDDEN TREASURE
1303 EAST UNIVERSITY BOULEVARD
TUCSON, AZ 85719

Dr. Ambrose L. Horn arrived at the Territorial University of Arizona in the late fall of 1893. It is said he arrived by way of the Tucson Livery Service Wagon and had a quick lesson in the ways of the dusty old West. Tying a silk handkerchief around his mouth and nose to filter the blowing desert sand, he soon found himself standing alone in front of Old Main.

Dr. Horn was known in the upper circles of the United States as a gifted surgeon and medical instructor. He was also known to be thrifty with his paycheck and bank accounts. The 1873 stock market crash lasted until 1878, and the stock market crashed once again from 1892 to 1893 in the United States. The public experienced financial panic, depression and economic meltdown while facing failed banks that left many citizens penniless.

Dr. Horn had lost a good part of his savings but was not as badly off as many others. Many people in this era decided they'd rather die by suicide or quietly disappear in the middle of the night than face family, friends and business acquaintances with the reality of bankruptcy.

The doctor's employment at the Territorial University of Arizona proved to be a good move financially, and the funds in his bank account increased rather steadily. But his memories of financial crashes, bank failures and public panics played over and over in the back of his mind and left him with a weary thought that banks and businesses could fail again if citizens were not careful.

A bird's-eye view postcard of the University of Arizona's campus. *Wikimedia.*

Janitors and several night owl students on campus began noticing what they thought was Dr. Horn on several late-night occasions digging in and around what was then the many cactus gardens located around the dark, shadowy twenty-acre desert grounds of the college.

Professors in the 1800s were often labeled eccentric, so the early rumors and matter of the doctor's late-night activities quickly passed though the gossiping students as a joke, and in time, most had forgotten Dr. Horn's unusual habits. Then one late stormy night in 1894, two members of the football team were walking around campus after an evening of drinking what was nicknamed Tucson's Red Eye Whiskey.

(In the 1800s, Tucson's Red Eye Whiskey often arrived in the city in large wooden barrels as a cheaper and clear grain alcohol liquid. To dress it up and give it a dark, expensive whiskey look, the local saloonkeepers would drop a couple handfuls of rusty old nails into the barrels to darken the color of the clear liquid, and within a few hours, it would have that popular dark amber whiskey look.)

On the walk back to the campus, the two football players spotted the dark, shadowy figure of a man off in the distance, mysteriously stooped over and hard at work near the middle of what is now the University of Arizona's mall area. At that time, it was a very large and well-manicured cactus garden.

As the two athletes came closer, they could barely make out the figure way out in the distance in front of them. But it was, without a doubt, the esteemed professor Dr. Ambrose L. Horn stooped, attentively looking at the ground and tamping down some earth with a small hand trowel that was normally used by the school's landscapers.

Not wanting to be caught with whiskey on their breaths and suffer demerits on their football team record, the two fraternity brothers quietly—and very quickly—changed their course and slipped away into the night unnoticed. Three days later, the two students were unable to ignore their secret any longer. On a moonlit night, both of the treasure hunters returned to the spot where they had observed the professor mysteriously digging under the cover of the desert's darkness.

The dirt on the ground was still fairly soft. But when the soil refused to budge, one of the students pulled out his small pocketknife and began digging deeper. He soon found, buried about twelve inches below the surface of the dirt, a small leather pouch with a thin lead liner inside.

The fraternity brothers opened the pouch and could not believe their eyes! To their surprise, the leather pouch was filled with gold in the form of ten-dollar, twenty-dollar and fifty-five-dollar gold pieces struck by the United States Mint!

The two students dashed back to their fraternity and roused the rest of their fraternity buddies with the strange news of their discovery. The group started devising their plans to secretly search for more of Professor Horn's hidden cache of gold coins.

However, none of the fraternity members had a clue that the mysterious Dr. Horn had witnessed the two young football players dig up and walk away with the leather pouch that he had so diligently buried that dark evening on the campus. The fraternity members could not imagine the horrendous surprise the good Dr. Horn was planning for all of them.

The crafty doctor remained quiet and waited for the right moment to get even. The annual Tucson Cotillion Dance was one of the most popular social events in town and was held each year in downtown Tucson. It was a great opportunity for the eligible young girls from the community's elite and wealthy families to connect with the handsome and intelligent men attending the University of Arizona. One of the requirements for the male college students to attend the event was that one of the school's own doctors had to perform a simple health exam to ensure the students were in good health.

Dr. Horn made his move. He made arrangements so that he would be the school doctor assigned to perform the exams on the young men. On the morning of the exams, most of the athletes and students at the school began to show up along with the fraternity brothers.

One local young man sat patiently in a chair in Dr. Horn's office. He was not a student but the son of a prominent Tucson businessman and a patient of Dr. Horn who happened to be seeking treatment for diphtheritic laryngitis. The doctor invited him to come in that day for his follow-up checkup.

Unknowingly, the student quickly infected all the fraternity brothers with his highly infectious disease. Diphtheritic laryngitis caused those who caught it to experience laryngitis, sexual impotence and a slight fever—not to mention vomiting and diarrhea. The small group of fraternity members who did attempt to attend the dance (despite their strange and abrupt illness) lasted only a few minutes before they were forced to dash out of the building with embarrassingly dark stains on the seats of their white dress pants, socks and shoes.

Dr. Horn had the last laugh and was satisfied with his act of revenge. Once again, the professor began the practice of burying his pouches of gold and silver coins around the campus on dark, moonless nights due to his distrust of banks.

Dr. Ambrose L. Horn died suddenly of a heart attack one afternoon while teaching a medical class. Although the grounds of the University of Arizona campus have changed many times over the years, only a few of his mysterious pouches of treasure have been discovered. They are usually found during campus construction projects, with the last pouch discovered in 2020.

The remaining pouches of gold and silver coins would now be considered highly valuable and are rumored to still be scattered all over the campus. The treasure would be quite a bonanza for some lucky person. The elusive professor's use of a thin lead liner in the pouches could be the reason they have remained hidden below the earth after all these years. But they could resurface during the next landscaping project! Happy hunting!

BEAR DOWN GYM
1428 EAST UNIVERSITY BOULEVARD
TUCSON, AZ 85721

The University of Arizona's battle cry, "Bear Down," echoes the final words of a dying twenty-two-year-old, spoken on Thursday, October 18, 1926. He was a popular student leader and talented athlete who often trained in what was then the newly built Men's Gymnasium (as the Bear Down Gym was originally named).

Bear Down Gym is a two-story brick structure noted for its curved roof; large, semicircular terra-cotta entrance; and deeply recessed entry with copper-clad window frames. The building is topped with a slightly projecting cornice that includes terra-cotta detailing. The exposed bowstring truss system is a notable interior feature.

In 1925, John "Button" Byrd Salmon was the president of the student body, the varsity football team's starting quarterback and team captain and a three-year catcher for the baseball team. He was extremely popular with his teammates, coaches, fellow students and the citizens of Tucson—and of course, all the young ladies in town swooned over his handsome looks!

John was born in Texas on October 22, 1902, and grew up with his parents and siblings in the rough-and-tumble town of Bisbee, Arizona. Nicknamed Button by his family for his small frame (he was five feet, eight inches tall and weighed 145 pounds) and extraordinarily impish good looks, his wild, curly hair and freckles inspired his teammates to tag him with yet another nickname, the "Leaping Tuna."

On the day after the 1926 season's big opening football game, John "Button" Byrd Salmon was driving at a very high rate of speed on his way back from Phoenix in his Ford Model T with one of his fraternity buddies and a young girl when he overcorrected on a treacherous curve and hit a dirt

University of Arizona's Bear Down Gym. *Wikimedia.*

berm along the side of the road near Picacho Peak, Arizona. His car flipped several times and crashed down in a deep ravine. He was pinned underneath the wreckage for hours before help could arrive. The other two passengers were ejected from the car and suffered only a few deep cuts and bruises.

But young Salmon was not so lucky. He suffered a severed spinal cord injury that left him paralyzed from the neck down. Dr. Victor Melsor, a well-respected and talented Tucson surgeon, performed a long, eight-hour surgery on Button at the Southern Methodist Hospital in Tucson, but the spinal injury was just too severe. John "Button" Byrd Salmon died two weeks later on October 18, 1926, at the hospital.

On the morning of October 18, 1926, Button gave a final message to his coach and football and baseball teammates. Salmon's coach, "Pop" McKale, who had been visiting the wounded player every day for the thirteen days at the hospital, was talking to Button when the injured young man whispered, "Pop, come closer…tell them…tell the team to Bear Down." The nurse who was attending the young man noted that Salmon breathed in one last breath and died peacefully at 10:32 a.m.

Later that night, Pop returned from the hospital and began working at his office desk in Bear Down Gym. At about 10:00 p.m., the ghost of John "Button" Byrd Salmon, wearing his football jersey, appeared to him at the doorway of his office and began walking toward the exhausted coach. The apparition uttered only two words: "Bear Down!"

All classes at the university were canceled on the day of Salmon's funeral, which was held at the campus's auditorium. A three-mile-long funeral procession of Model Ts, Model As, horse-drawn wagons and folks on horseback slowly made its way north of town to Evergreen Cemetery.

Other employees, janitors and students have reported encountering the spirit of a short young man in a well-used 1920s football uniform moving throughout various areas of the gym.

Shortly after December 7, 1941, and the outbreak of World War II, Bear Down Gym was taken over by the U.S. War Department as barracks for five hundred young students as they went through their expedited Naval Indoctrination School before being shipped off to war. Many of the young sailors and officers who trained there gave their lives to the war effort and never returned. It is said that their spirits still frequent Bear Down Gym, looking to start where their young lives left off—back where they were vibrant young students.

HOLAWAY ELEMENTARY SCHOOL
3500 NORTH CHERRY AVENUE
TUCSON, AZ 85719

Francis Owen Holaway Elementary School is located on the corner of Cherry and Prince Avenues in central Tucson. Founded in 1957, the school is a proud member of the Amphitheater School District. Holaway supports students from kindergarten to the fifth grade and has both a typical and special needs preschool located near its campus.

Francis Holaway was a member of the district school board for fifteen years, from 1931 to 1946. He was a guiding force behind the erection of the Amphitheater Junior High School building in 1938. A native of Louisiana, Holaway lived in Tucson for thirty-two years. He was a disabled veteran of World War I, before which he taught grade school and served as a principal. Holaway passed away in January 1955 at the age of fifty-five. He was buried in the Masonic section of Evergreen Cemetery in Tucson. The ghost at Holaway Elementary is said to be his spirit.

There have been several sightings of Mr. Holaway slowly walking down the school's hallways. The janitor at the school reported that one night, while he was alone in the building, emptying the trash and cleaning the floors, he looked up from his duties and saw a mysterious man walking down the hall directly in front of him. This man was checking all the classroom doors to make sure they were locked. The janitor didn't realize that what he was seeing at the time was a ghost, so he shouted out to the man to get his attention. When the janitor received a somewhat mumbled response, he began to walk firmly toward the man. That is when the janitor realized that what he thought was a man was merely a ghost. The gentleman, who resembled F.O. Holaway, disappeared before his eyes.

7
PINAL COUNTY

OLD SUPERIOR HIGH SCHOOL
98 HIGHSCHOOL AVENUE
SUPERIOR, AZ 85273

Among the earliest inhabitants of the Superior area were the Natives of the Apache tribe, the Pascua Yaqui tribe and the Tohono O'odham Nation. During the American Indian Wars of the 1870s, a company of Apache horsemen were ambushed by the U.S. Cavalry. After losing fifty men, the Apache retreated up a mountain located within the site that would become Superior. The defeated Apache warriors leaped to their deaths to escape being captured by the U.S. Army, so the mountain became known as the Apache Leap Mountain.

It wasn't long before prospectors arrived in search of gold. Prospector Charles Mason staked the area's first claims in 1875. In 1880, the Silver Queen Mining Company was organized, and in 1882, the town of Hastings was founded and platted.

Owners of a successful silver mine named their mine Lake Superior. These stockholders were originally from Michigan. The Lake Superior Mine was the main contributor to the area's economy. In 1902, the community changed its name from Hastings to Superior, after the mine.

William Boyce Thompson bought the old Silver Queen Mine in 1910, and by 1912, the new Magma Copper Company was up and running the operations of the Silver Queen Mine. The Magma Copper Company soon became one Arizona's greatest copper producers after the silver vein of the Silver Queen Mine dried up and ran out.

One of the positive consequences of World War I, as well as World War II, was the increased demand for copper. The town of Superior flourished. However, by the 1980s, the main mining operations were moved to the nearby town of Miami. The Magma Copper Company's smelter, with the exception of the historic smelter stack, was sadly demolished.

The high school was designed by Tucson architect H.O. Jaastad, and in August 1924, the Superior Construction Company was awarded the contract for the construction of a new $63,000 high school. The construction was supervised by the new principal, Professor O.A. Anderson, and the school was expected to be completed in ninety working days and ready for students in the fall. This would give Superior a fully accredited high school.

Dr. A.O. Neal, the registrar of the University of Arizona, was the main speaker at the February 1925 dedication program of the completed new school. Superior High School celebrated its first graduating class in 1929

The historic Superior High School. *Author's collection.*

Superior High School, built in 1925. *Author's collection.*

and honored its last graduating class in 2000. A new school was opened in another area of Superior.

The former school is now a residential space. Many of the classrooms inside have been converted to guest suites. The school's office has become a casual living room. The home economics building is used as the home's kitchen, and the former school library serves as the media room. The old gymnasium and locker rooms are still intact, including functioning bleachers and Superior Panthers pawprints decorating the walls. All this and more present an assembly of old and new—much like the town of Superior.

The paranormal team Crossing Over Paranormal Society was fortunate to gain permission for a ghost investigation in the historic Superior High School. The team came to explore the many paranormal claims from the townspeople, which state the location is extremely haunted. Folks who reside in Superior have heard things, seen things and felt things at the school they cannot explain.

The team spent several hours in the catacombs of the basement, exploring various hallways and empty rooms. Nearly all of them had an uneasy feeling in one long, narrow storage room.

"We investigated the basement area in depth," explained COPS crew leader Jay Yates. "The basement is where they stored the gym equipment when it was operational. I saw a dark mass run at me while Marie [Yates] was filming. She saw and captured the same oddity on video."

Yates continued, "We moved on to a crawl space down there that had a low clearance. Marie and I both felt something we could not actually see rush right though us. It made it kind of scary, as it was super dark and much cooler in the area. In that same crawl space, we also saw shadow play— movement within the shadows. We were told that area was the original section of the school before what you see was built on top of it."

Jay noted that they could hear residual sounds of basketballs hitting the floor, as if some unseen basketball game was in play. They had some intelligent interaction using their EMF equipment.

"Marie and I gave chase to what appeared to be a man on the school grounds." Jay reported, "We heard him talking as he was running away— either to draw us to him or to get away. We ended up in a dead end behind the school, where he seemingly just vanished!"

No one knows the identity of the mysterious spirit. Could it be a former teacher or student who is dedicated to the school? A construction worker or former maintenance employee? A miner who once toiled in the nearby Silver Queen Mine? Or perhaps a Native still protecting the land? Perhaps someday, the spirit will be dismissed from its eternal ties to the school.

FIRST AVENUE ELEMENTARY SCHOOL
914 WEST FIRST AVENUE
SAN MANUEL, AZ 85631

First Avenue Elementary School in San Manuel offers classes for more than 285 students in pre-kindergarten through the third grade. The school employs a psychologist, a reading coach, a speech therapist, a nurse, paraprofessionals, classroom teachers and other support staff members. It conducts classes in art, English, math, science and social studies. First Avenue Elementary School is a part of the Mammoth-San Manuel Unified School District, which governs various elementary, middle and high schools. The district's schools host Memorial Day celebrations and parent-teacher conferences.

First Avenue
Elementary School
sign in San Manuel.
Wikimedia.

This urban legend revolves around the ghost of a young boy who is rumored to have died after falling off the merry-go-round and hitting his head while being crushed by the apparatus itself. The ghost appears to be holding his head and cries before vanishing.

A member of one San Manuel family claimed, "I have seen him—and not only did I see him, but I also saw the merry-go-round playground equipment move on its own."

8

SANTA CRUZ COUNTY

PATAGONIA ELEMENTARY SCHOOL
100 SCHOOL STREET
PATAGONIA, AZ 85624

Patagonia Elementary School sits on a hill near the foot of Red Mountain and has a breathtaking view of Patagonia. It was built in 1914, after the previous school building was consumed by fire in 1912. The building, with large windows and pressed tin ceilings, now houses the Patagonia Museum. It boasts a bell tower that once announced the start of classes each day.

The school was funded by the sales of bonds. So much money was successfully raised that the town's committee hired a Nogales architect (O.J. Olmstead) to design the brick schoolhouse. Patagonia Elementary School was built on a hill that was known in the surrounding Patagonia area to have been a Native lookout. On the hill, a person can see for miles in every direction. Many pieces of Native pottery and artifacts have been found there—including bones. A former principal of the school declared he once discovered a complete skeleton on the hill. University of Arizona scientists confirmed the remains were those of a Native, and they were later reburied. Other explorers claim to have found skeletons as well—but on examination, these skeletons are in fact bone pieces in burial pots that were placed in the ground after cremation, which was the practice of the

Hohokam tribe. The Hohokam thrived in the Patagonia area from about 1050 CE to 1450 CE.

The historic schoolhouse, nicknamed Old Main, was one of the longest-operating schools in Arizona (1914–2014). The campus had been a hub of the Patagonia community for over one hundred years. Old Main was once the central gathering location for the community. Old Main was the education center for generations of Patagonia students. Every class of departing fifth graders was featured in a photograph taken on the front steps of the old schoolhouse.

The old school is no longer filled with children, but many alumni remember the hardwood floors of the four classrooms and the lack of indoor restrooms or a lunchtime cafeteria. On cool, breezy days, many teachers held their classes outdoors, much to the students' delight. Both students and teachers alike loved the school's peaceful location and considered it a sort of "utopia on the hill."

Former students of Patagonia Elementary School have witnessed the apparition of a tall, dark man in the hallways of the old schoolhouse. They noted they could see his body, only legs, arms, a torso and shoulders. The body had no head!

Patagonia Elementary School. *Wikimedia.*

In the late 1970s or early 1980s, a group of schoolboys spent their recess exploring the playground behind the schoolhouse. They were searching for historic heirlooms, relics and treasure. Much to their delight, they began uncovering pottery shards, arrowheads and even a piece of pottery in perfect condition. All was fun and games until one of the boys thought he struck pay dirt; in fact, he uncovered a severed human skull and screamed. The other boys gathered around him and marveled at his find. But something didn't feel right. They decided the right thing to do was contact local officials. These officials immediately fenced off the area to curious schoolboys and conducted an archaeological dig. The relics were identified, tagged and stowed away for safekeeping.

Could this be the skull of the headless Native seen searching the hallways of the old schoolhouse? Similar to the headless horseman in "The Legend of Sleepy Hollow," is this Native man doomed to search for his head for eternity?

Patagonia Elementary School was closed in 2014 but still holds a claim for being one of the longest-operating schools in Arizona. Fortunately, the historic building has been saved, restored and converted into the Patagonia Museum. There are various exhibits in the museum where guests can learn about the mining and ranching history of the town. The museum is full of historic maps, photographs and several anecdotes from the locals who share the stories of early life in Patagonia.

Among the exhibits is a tree stump that once belonged to the town's jail tree. The aged stump is mounted on a stand with a rusty chain hanging to the ground. Notorious prisoners were shackled to the tree whenever the Patagonia Jail's cells were overcrowded. Are the energies of these broken men emitted throughout the old schoolhouse museum?

One of the museum's most interesting exhibits is the Patagonia Jail Cave. There are close-up photographs of the cave to view in the museum, and later, out in the parking lot, you can find the black triangle on a white metal railing from where you can look out and actually see the cave.

Stay a few minutes late at closing time, when the museum's volunteer docent rings the old school bell to signal the end of another day of school at Old Main. But have all the students moved on to a higher education, or have some of them remained after school?

RUBY SCHOOLHOUSE
(FROM I-19 TAKE EXIT 48 FOR ARIAVACA ROAD, DRIVE TWENTY-THREE MILES AND TURN LEFT ON SOUTH RUBY ROAD.)
RUBY, AZ

Ruby is a ghost town in Santa Cruz County. It was founded as a mining town in Bear Valley, originally named Montana Camp because the miners were mining at the foot of Montana Peak. Mining there began around 1877. The Montana Mine produced gold, silver, lead, zinc and copper. At its peak in the mid-1930s, Ruby had a population of about 1,200.

On April 11, 1912, the mining camp's general store owner, Julius Andrews, established the post office. Andrews named the post office Ruby, after his wife, Lille B. Ruby Andrews, and the mining camp was soon known as Ruby. The Ruby Post Office was established in 1912 and was discontinued on May 31, 1941.

The most prosperous period for Ruby came in the late 1920s and 1930s, when the Eagle-Pitcher Mining Company operated the mine and upgraded the camp. From 1934 to 1937, the Montana Mine was the leading lead and zinc producer in Arizona. In 1936, it was third in silver production. The mine was closed in 1940, and by the end of 1941, Ruby was abandoned.

Ruby lives up to its reputation as one of the two best-preserved mining ghost towns in Arizona. (The other is the Vulture Mine near Wickenburg.) Ruby's attractions today include approximately twenty-five buildings under roof, including the jail, residential houses, the school with a nearby playground, shop buildings and mining workings. Ruby is located entirely on private property, and there is a charge for admission to the site.

Between 1920 and 1922, the town of Ruby and the surrounding areas were the scene of three double homicides known as the Ruby Murders. These deaths led to one of the largest manhunts in the history of the Southwest.

Ruby's location so close to the border with Mexico made it a prime target for the robberies and acts of violence that were common during that period. Sadly, this location contributed to the two separate, horrendous double murder sprees. Both times, the victims were the proprietors of the Ruby Mercantile, the largest and most profitable general store in the area. John and Alexander Fraser were killed in a robbery by two Mexican bandits on February 27, 1920. The brothers had owned the mercantile for only eleven days.

Ruby Schoolhouse view. *Author's collection.*

Husband and wife Frank and Myrtle Pearson bought the store after the Fraser murders, figuring a tragedy like that could never happen again. Unfortunately, on August 26, 1921, it did. In a similar brutal and vicious crime, the mercantile was robbed by seven banditos. The Pearsons were gunned down after Myrtle was beaten to knock out the five gold crowns off her teeth. This all happened in full view of the Pearsons' daughter Margaret and her young aunts, Elizabeth and Irene. They were able to hide, escape injury and report the crime.

There were massive hunts with posse chases, shootouts, escapes, big rewards, dead-or-alive wanted posters, army troops, federal agents and the first use of airplanes in a law enforcement manhunt.

Justice caught up with the two Fraser murderers. One was killed in a shootout. The other was imprisoned in Mexico for another murder but was never held accountable for the Fraser killings.

Of the seven killers involved in the Pearson murders, one was hanged and another served a life term in prison in Arizona. The rest were never caught.

The townspeople were so frightened that they canceled school in Ruby. The county superintendent declared that no female teacher would be assigned as long as there were no soldiers at Ruby. And it was very doubtful that any male teacher would be sent there as long as there was no protection from bandit raids.

Most people will agree that Ruby is haunted due to its bloody history. Many visitors have encountered spirits at the Ruby Schoolhouse throughout the years. The school was a three-room stucco adobe, and there was a large tent out back for the student overflow. The teachers who taught grades one through eight lived in the back room of the school. Some guests agree that the twenty-foot-tall playground slide seems to be the scariest location on the property. The deteriorating slide has no protective railing up its steep steps. The slide was made of sheet metal with exposed rivets, and the side rails were made of wood. Ouch!

One visitor traveled to Ruby all alone. She assumed other people would be exploring the site as well since she was visiting on a weekend. But the woman was the only soul there aside from the border patrol agent she had passed a few miles back. The school was remote, and the curious visitor could not locate the caretaker to pay the entrance fee before entering the gate. The solo woman had driven two hours on a very rough road and could see the town peeking around the turns. She just couldn't turn back. She debated whether she was being brave or just plain stupid, but she continued her quest and drove up to a caretaker's trailer, only to find no

Ruby School's slide. *Pinterest.*

one inside. She drove around for a little bit, determined not to get out since she was by herself.

Then she saw the old schoolhouse and the piano sitting just inside its doorway. It was as though the ivory keys were calling to her. Just beyond the school were the ruins of the general store. The explorer just wanted to touch the piano and glance into the school for a few minutes. Carefully, she exited the car and began walking toward the old piano. She clearly heard footsteps behind her in the dry grass, and she quickly turned around. No one was there. She walked a little farther and heard the footsteps nearer and felt a presence. Nervous, she whipped around, positive there was someone nearby. Again, there was no one.

She bravely made it to the doorway where the piano stood. The footsteps behind her were now very loud and clear, and they sounded like they were caused by a person, not a critter. The dreaded feeling of not being alone was disquieting. The woman felt there was more than one person in the building. It was exhilarating to be near these eternal people. She blocked out her fear momentarily to reach in and play a few keys on the piano—*bang, bang*—and then the feeling of not being alone overtook her once again. She bolted out, peeked in the windows and snapped a few pictures. She ran to her car, locked the doors and drove away.

Yes, Ruby is haunted! The energies the woman met were not mean, just very curious. She said she will return, but she will never go alone ever again!

Another visitor to Ruby and the schoolhouse noted, "Yes, in the schoolhouse, by the piano, something or someone is there. It was almost as if there was a child in the corner."

Ruby School's chalkboard. *Author's collection.*

One explorer had this to say about Ruby,

> *With its bloody history, it would come as no surprise if this old ghost town is haunted. The legend tells of the mercantile having been built over an old padre's grave. After the first double murder, while a law enforcement officer was investigating, he was told by an old-time local that there was a curse on the building. The old-timer said, "Old Tio Pedro died years ago. He predicted evil for the occupants of the mercantile cause it was built over an old padre's grave." The investigator confirmed the superstition with the local police officer, who informed the investigator that "the legend was common among the Mexicans of the area."*

The man added,

> *I don't consider myself to be a ghost hunter, but frequently I just sort of run into them—and on a rare occasion, I get a glimpse of one. We had wandered through the Ruby buildings for an hour or so, and as we made our way back out, we decided to stop at the old Ruby School.*
>
> *It is a building left back in time. It still had the historic chalkboards, as well as some of the old desks and furnishings. I had a heavy feeling in my chest that there was a spirit in the room with us. I walked into the adjoining classroom, where my friend was taking photographs. We both heard footsteps in the other room. We dashed back into the room, but there was no one there. Now, we started hearing footsteps in the room, and we just left. Again, we looked, but no one was there! I am sure that something paranormal was in the schoolhouse. It just happens to be close to the old Ruby mercantile, so who knows?*

Several years ago, the MVD Ghostchasers paranormal team was asked to do a speaking engagement at a local university. One of the guests in the audience told them about the quaint little ghost town called Ruby in southern Arizona. They learned it was the location of a brutal murder scene back in the 1920s. A road trip and investigation of Ruby became a "must do" on the group's list of Arizona's haunted places to visit.

This author remembers the day's misadventure:

> *A senior member, Roger, made the necessary arrangements with the owners of the town site. One weekend in February 1999, eleven team members, including myself, caravanned to southern Arizona and drove the treacherous*

road to Ruby. Three pickup trucks, one compact car and one motorcycle crept along the dusty, narrow highway. Suddenly, we came to a spot in the road that was completely flooded with water. We feared we would have to turn around and go back. The men hopped out of the vehicles and assessed the perils of driving through the dangerous waters. Bravely, we decided to make a run for it. Campers nearby cheered as each vehicle—and motorcycle— drove through the puddle of water at full speed.

The dirt road narrowed down to one lane, making it almost impossible to see what was around the next bend. We held our breath as the vehicles twisted around the curvy mountain road. Gary dodged boulders that had fallen in the roadway, making the journey into what one would call an obstacle course.

Before we knew it, we were at the gates that open into Ruby. The caretaker was sitting in his pickup truck, waiting for our arrival. "You're late!" he scolded in a stern tone of voice.

We explained that there had been a flooded roadblock while the man reviewed the sign-in sheet on his clipboard and collected the entrance fee. We each signed a waiver stating we would not sue if any of us were injured or fell in an old mineshaft. I noticed the scruffy-looking man had a terrible-looking, puss-filled sore on his bruised and swollen face.

We drove through the gate entrance, and suddenly, the once-thriving town of Ruby was in view. The site of the vacant houses speckling the hillside was awe-inspiring. It was a place time had forgotten. It was also one of the best-preserved ghost towns we had ever investigated. At one time, 150 children attended the schoolhouse, and over 300 men worked in the Montana Silver Mine.

We had a great time exploring the old jail, schoolhouse, store and several old homes. We walked down to the cemetery and peered into some of the old mineshafts. The ladies asked team member Stu to prop open the window of one of the vacant houses with a stick from a tree so we could photograph the inside of the home. That way, we could keep a safe distance outside the old building and still get the photographs we desired. Photograph opportunities were everywhere we looked! We marveled over the old mining equipment that was still sitting where it had been abandoned so many years ago.

What we didn't know was that our afternoon visit was being observed under the watchful eye of the strange-looking caretaker. He sat in his pickup truck parked at the top of a Ruby hillside. He watched every move we made with his trusty binoculars. He approached two of the group's members, Shiela and Chris, in the parking lot. He threatened them that he was going

Ruby School's classroom. *Pinterest.*

to call the sheriff because he had seen someone steal a window out of one of the abandoned houses. Shiela frantically explained to the man that we never take anything but photographs during their sessions. We gathered in the parking lot, where the caretaker was demanding to search our vehicles for the missing window. Stu tried to explain that he had only propped the window open with a stick and offered to walk back to the building with the caretaker to show him.

I suddenly envisioned the team being marched inside the old concrete jail while the team and I awaited our doom with the country sheriff. The group being crowded in that tiny, dark jail with the thick block walls seemed intimidating. What if we were left there for several hours—or even worse, several days! Then I remembered that Roger used to carry what we jokingly called a mini arsenal in the back of his old beat-up pickup truck. He toted enough guns and ammo for us to fight off a small revolution if need be. I decided we should simply tell our captor that Roger needed to go to his truck to find his diabetes medicine. Roger could then unlock his truck, grab an armload of the guns and ammo, trot back to the jail and toss us guns so we could shoot our way out of bloody Ruby like the A-Team. My imagination had gone wild—as wild as the dream sequence of this paragraph!

But fortunately, it didn't come to that. Our nervous group convinced the caretaker we were just a humble band of ghost hunters and would never think of stealing anything. At sundown, the weary caretaker escorted us back to the property gate—and to freedom!

About two days later, we read the newspaper and learned the real reason for the caretaker's odd accusations. The news story stated that earlier that day (before MVD Ghostchasers had arrived in Ruby), the caretaker had been bitten on the face by a rabid skunk. That explained the horrible sore on his face. He had to be rushed to the hospital a few hours after the team left that evening. No wonder he was hallucinating!

9
YAVAPAI COUNTY

CLEAR CREEK CHURCH (SCHOOLHOUSE)
2910 SOUTH OLD CHURCH ROAD
CAMP VERDE, AZ 86322

The Clear Creek Church was constructed between 1898 and 1903 and is located on Clear Creek Road three and a half miles southeast of Camp Verde, Arizona. It was listed in the National Register of Historic Places in 1975.

It was built using limestone blocks quarried from Hayfield Wash on the Middle Verde River near the White Hills. The blocks ranged from ten by thirteen inches to twelve by eighteen inches in size. The building in plan is forty by twenty-five feet. It boasts a high gable roof.

The builders placed in the cornerstone of the building a Bible and a five-dollar gold piece. It is said the gold piece was chiseled away in the 1920s. The little church served the local Methodist community until 1913, when the congregation built a new church closer to town, and the structure was repurposed as the town's one-room schoolhouse.

A May 8, 1940 newspaper talked about the Clear Creek School's graduation exercises. The diplomas were presented to Paul Wright and Bill Simpson. There were brief addresses given by Margaret Hallett, the school's principal, and Herman Schweikart of the Camp Verde High School faculty, and a presentation of two plays was featured on the program.

Left: Camp Verde Clear Creek's 1898 school/church. *Pinterest*.

Opposite: Camp Verde Clear Creek's school/church, restored between 1975 and 1979. *Courtesy of Deb Wilber*.

The structure was later used as a cannery during World War II. In 1946, the dilapidated building was abandoned. It was eventually donated to the Camp Verde Historical Society, whose gracious volunteers restored it between 1975 and 1979. Today, it is occasionally open for tours, weddings and other functions.

Over a dozen star gazers traveled up to the Camp Verde area on Friday, May 23, 2014, seeking the clear skies in great anticipations of a majestic meteor shower. Several members of various paranormal organizations attended the event. The paranormal team Verde Valley Spirit Seekers organized the meteor watch. Scientists reported that early on Saturday, Earth would pass by debris from Comet 209P/Linear. The dusty debris is what would create the meteor shower. Scientists believed the shower could possibly produce a few hundred shooting stars per minute.

North American sky-gazers were promised the best views. The shower would peak from around 2:00 a.m. until nearly dawn. Comet 209P/Linear is a dim comet that orbits the sun every five years. It was discovered in 2004. Meteor showers vary in intensity, as some produce more meteors than others.

It was predicted that during this meteor shower, all of Comet 209P/Liners's debris trails from 1803 to 1924 would intersect Earth's orbit, producing hundreds of meteors per hour. Aside from a cloudy night, a meteor watcher's worst enemy is a bright moon that can wash out all but the brightest meteors. However, the moon on the night of May 23, 2014, was not present until about 3:45 a.m. and did not affect the meteor shower.

The group gathered at the Clear Creek Cemetery and set up their watch in a circle of chairs near the grave site of a longtime friend and fellow ghost hunter, Judy Valencia. Ghost stories and theories were discussed as the evening grew dark and began to feel much colder. After a stroll around the historic cemetery and an investigation of the Clear Creek Church, the group continued their sky watch. Only a few small meteors were detected in the distance, with one large fireball falling star witnessed close by.

A handful of investigators decided to tough it out and spent the remainder of the evening and early morning hours in the shelter of the warm Clear Creek Church. Settling for the comfort of sleeping bags along the hard wooden pews, the night owls continued their EVP sessions, which had been initiated earlier in the evening, and watched the moon rise in the eastern sky at about 3:45 a.m.

Footsteps, cold spots and the sounds of children (remember the old church was also used as a schoolhouse from time to time) were experienced, and the data was analyzed and documented.

Camp Verde boasts the historic Clear Creek Church (schoolhouse) and Clear Creek Cemetery. These are great places to discover and learn about the history of Verde Valley. The cemetery covers five acres of land and was once site of the earliest settlements in the valley. The charming little cemetery is the final resting spot for some of these early pioneers. It is also known to have a few lively spirits.

The early settlement, where Clear Creek meets with the Verde River, consisted of farming families. The easy access to water and the rich soil provided the small community with fine crops. Clear Creek is near the site of the first Forte Verde—or Fort Lincoln, as it was named—and was occupied by soldiers from Prescott. These men came to protect the settlers from the Yavapai and Apache Indians who had earlier claims to the rich farmland.

The Clear Creek Church (schoolhouse) and Cemetery are just a few miles away from the present city center of Camp Verde. The site of the fort has also moved up to the other bank of the river over the years. The cemetery remains a big part of Camp Verde history and is still in use today. With new housing developments popping up all around the cemetery, the church and schoolhouse are barely out in the countryside these days.

The earliest recorded burial is dated 1868. A despondent seventeen-year-old girl, Maggie Farrell, in the settlement died by suicide and was laid to rest in what is now the oldest section of the cemetery. Maggie's grave is marked only by a metal name plate. No monument honors her sad, short life.

One can hardly miss the Wingfield family plot. A botched robbery in 1899 at the old Wingfield Mercantile claimed the lives of Robert Mac Rodgers and Clinton Wingfield. Rodgers was shot by the assailant near the doorway of the store. Clinton Wingfield, hearing the gunshots, came out of a back room and was also shot. The bullet entered his chest and became lodged in his spine, paralyzing him instantly. Townsfolk carried him back across the street to the main room of the stage depot building and gave him medical

Camp Verde Clear Creek's school/church, built between 1898 and 1903. *Courtesy of Deb Wilber.*

treatment. He died two hours later in front of the fireplace. Wingfield and Rodger's graves stand side by side in the cement-bordered plot.

Deb Wilber, one of the founders of Verde Valley Spirit Seekers, has spent a lot of time investigating both the Clear Creek Church (schoolhouse) and the nearby cemetery. Deb has a few photographs with what looks like a mysterious mist floating in the cemetery. One evening, her nephew was carrying a cell sensor, and the alarm started going off. Deb snapped a picture of him, and he had that strange mist surrounding him, too.

129

Her son James recorded an EVP that sounded like a group of children shrieking or laughing in the distance. There was no one else around. For a long time, the mysterious laughter and voices of unseen children did not make a lot of sense to the seasoned paranormal investigators. But when it happened again across the road from the old Clear Creek Church (schoolhouse), the investigators came to reason who might be haunting the area. Did the schoolchildren romp among the tombstones in the quaint little cemetery? Can some of these restless spirits be seeking redemption to pass to the world beyond? Visit on an evening when the meteors intensify the spirit energy and learn for yourself.

SPIRITED CHILDREN OF THE COTTONWOOD CIVIC CENTER
805 NORTH MAIN STREET
COTTONWOOD, AZ 86326

The MVD Ghostchasers and the Verde Valley Spirit Seekers presented a paranormal workshop in Clarkdale and Cottonwood, Arizona, in July 2012. The group of paranormal investigators and members from teams across the state visited several potentially haunted locations. They learned the history of these buildings and, in many cases, were able to conduct mini investigations or EVP sessions at some of the sites. One of these locations was the Cottonwood Civic Center.

When going into this particular location, the organizers did not consider it one of the major hot spots for hauntings. They did know the Women's Club of Cottonwood, which was organized to feed the hungry, raised money to build the Cottonwood Civic Center in 1939. The civic center, constructed of river rock, was built with labor provided by the Works Progress Administration (WPA) and served as the town's clubhouse. During World War II, the building was converted into temporary barracks for U.S. naval cadets.

The paranormal investigators, escorted by a member of Cottonwood's parks and recreation office, explored the basement and other areas of this unique building. Several of them found themselves backstage, where they decided to do a dowsing exercise backed up by a recorded EVP session.

Above: Cottonwood Civic Center. *Wikimedia*.

Right: A close-up of the Cottonwood Civic Center. *Courtesy of Deb Wilber.*

What happened next baffled the investigators. The ladies began asking the spirits the standard questions. A sensitive described "seeing" a spirit of a little girl wearing black Mary Jane shoes with white ankle socks who had been born in 1940. The voices of small children were later heard chattering in the background on the audio recorder of LIPS member Shelly. There were no children on the stage nor anywhere else in the building. There were no children in the investigating group. Finally, one of the women asked, "Do other people know you are here in this building besides us?" You can hear a sweet young child reply with a long, drawn-out, "No."

Why are there ghost children in the Cottonwood Civic Center? After a bit of research, we learned, according to a former Cottonwood–Oak Creek school superintendent, in 1878, the first school was established in Cottonwood and was located on the site where the Cottonwood Civic Center now proudly stands in Old Town. The former school was a rough stucco structure with only the bare minimum in the classroom: one blackboard, homemade seats and desks and a tin water bucket with one dipper for all to use. The adobe school had been used previously by soldiers sent from Fort Whipple to protect the town and the pioneers who were settling in the area.

Cottonwood Civic Center. *Courtesy of Deb Wilber.*

School was a happy place for the children of the West. It was where they socialized and had time to forget the chores and hard work waiting for them back home on their families' farms and ranches. Why wouldn't they want to return and frolic once more?

To see the location where the voices of ghost children at play are heard, visit the next event at the Cottonwood Civic Center.

JEROME HIGH SCHOOL
885 HAMPSHIRE AVENUE (HIGHWAY 89A)
JEROME, AZ 86331

The somewhat deserted Jerome High School building was the high school for the town of Jerome for several years. Its mascot was the Mucker. The massive building opened in 1923 and closed in 1951, when it was consolidated along with Clarkdale High School to make Mingus High School. When Cottonwood High School was later added, the school became known as Mingus Union High School, which was housed in Jerome from 1960 to 1975. That school's graduates are probably the only ones in the nation who can claim they have a degree from a ghost town!

Main Street Primary School was once a three-story school building. The second-story entrance, just off Highway 89A, remains as a ghostly reminder of the early school. The construction of the school began in 1913, and it was opened May 29, 1914, to honor its first three graduates. The building became inadequate almost immediately despite an $18,000 makeover. Another school was built in 1920 in Deception Gulch.

Following the decline in copper prices in 1932, the school board voted to close Main Street Primary School. In 1944, the building was sold for $606, and it was demolished in 1945. The retaining walls for the first floor and the steps to the playground were left intact. The steps to the third floor still lie across the middle retaining wall. The property was leased in 1964 and later sold to Joan Evens, a former teacher at Mingus Union High School.

Superintendent John O. Mullin and his family arrived in Jerome in 1918 to find the school properties consisted of the old Main Street Primary School, the old Jerome High School uptown below the United Verde Hospital (recently used for a city yard) and an old wooden grammar school that sat on

Jerome High School's front entrance. *Author's collection.*

a cement slab along Highway 89A. The total enrollment in 1918 comprised a mere 791 students. Due to the growth of the city, the peak enrollment in Jerome schools grew to 1,919 pupils in 1930 with a staff and faculty of 68.

As the copper town flourished, so did the schools. The main school building at Jerome High School had lecture rooms with sloping, tiered seats for presentations and demonstrations. There were large, fully equipped physics and chemistry labs. The home economics department boasted the latest in refrigerators, stoves and work counter space. The machine shops had the latest in power tools.

It was said the gymnasium and auditorium were works of art. The auditorium seated seven hundred and was fitted with a projection room comparable to those of local movie theaters and offered the latest in visual aids, lectures and educational movies. No modern technique of instruction was neglected!

The gymnasium, housed in a separate building, cost $80,000 when it was constructed in 1937. It had an enormous gym, showers, locker rooms, equipment and massage rooms! Jerome High School boasted champion basketball and football teams.

John O. Mullen was the superintendent of schools in Jerome for thirty-one years before he retired in 1949. He passed away in his Jerome home in February 1954.

Currently, the former school building is being used to house artists' studios, light industry and private business, and it provides paranormal investigators a location to study ghostly phenomena.

One person who toured the old high school said, "We didn't get any names or voices at the high school, but there was some serious negative energy in the basement and boys' locker room. Something did not want us down there. Our hearts felt like they might explode—they were racing so fast. My stomach got so tight that it literally hurt hours later. It was super creepy."

Another guest added, "We didn't get to play with the EMF meters. However, the feeling two of us had in the high school tells us that maybe we didn't need them. I witnessed 'a glimpse of a spirit girl.' Maybe she's still there. If so, tell 'Anna' hello."

A guest on another tour reported, "We had several spikes on the EMF meters, a couple of voices on the spirit boxes and my daughter said she felt the back pocket of her jeans tugged on in the boys' locker room of the old high school. My friends and I were constantly getting poked in the girls' locker room, and one could feel a spirit's breath near her."

Yet another added, "We learned some good history, but the paranormal stuff was super exciting! I was kind of a skeptic going into it, but when I saw the lights move and heard the voices, I knew it was real! I spoke with an Anne and Josh for quite some time in the high school auditorium balcony, and Josh said my daughter's name. My other daughter had a conversation with a Grace in the basement. She didn't want to talk to anyone other than her. It was so cool!"

Ginger Mason, a Jerome historian and tour guide with Ghost Town Tours Jerome, noted, "I have seen body parts in the High School during the tours. A shadow arm waved at me from the elbow down. I have also seen legs from the knees down wearing blue jeans and cowboy boots going up the stairs. I also heard someone running back and forth on the balcony—and that's with half the floor missing!"

Jerome High School's auditorium doors. *Author's collection.*

Ginger added, "A girl has been spotted just outside the girls' locker room, and I saw a shadow man in the girls' locker room as well. The only tragedy I know of is talk of a young lady that fell down the stairs to the stage and broke her neck and died a few days later. I believe the spirits are some of the Jerome townspeople who were former students of the high school. It's still abandoned for the most part."

Another paranormal investigator, Brian Evans, recalled his experience at the historic high school.

> *I decided to take my brother on a ghost hunt tour for his birthday back in 2015. We did the ghost hunt with Jerome Ghost Tours, and the guide escorted the group to the old Jerome High School and provided us with equipment such as a SB11 Spirit Box and a K2 Meter.*

I was in what was once the boys' locker room near where the showers used to be. I began to get some hits on the K2 Meter. My brother came into the room, and we had communications with the spirits almost immediately. About twenty minutes later, I ventured off on my own due to the tour being a bit crowded with several guests.

I was still manning the K2 meter, and my brother followed behind me about ten minutes later with the Spirit Box. As he walked through the doorway, he stopped and said, "I just felt my shirt tugged on!" Now, he was past the doorframe and inside the shower room. There was nothing he could have snagged his shirt on.

I took the K2 meter and held it near his shoulder and asked, "If there is anybody in here that tugged on my brother's shirt, can you stand next to him?" The meter light went from green to orange.

I then said, "You can touch him if you want!" My brother jumped and began to touch the back of his neck and nervously stated, "Something is touching me!" At the same time, the Spirit Box blurted, "Shiver!"

That was my first paranormal encounter, and I must say, most memorable!

The old Jerome High School could be one of the most haunted locations in the city. Harrison Karl, another seeker of the unknown, contacted me about his experience in the popular learning center.

On Valentine's Day 2019, my wife and I went to Jerome and stayed at the Grand Hotel. We had planned to take the Jerome ghost tour, but it rained all day and our tour was canceled. I told them I was an experienced ghost investigator, and we were looking forward to investigating some of the ghost city's haunts.

They drew me a map and sent us over to the old high school. On our first visit, there were people still inside the building. Any audio evidence would have been contaminated. We decided to hit it early—about one o'clock in the morning. Once inside the building, we decided to separate. She went to the bottom floor, and I went up to the third floor. It was quiet until I stopped to rest on the stairwell and used the tactic of not asking any questions—thus allowing the spirit to take over the mic.

It was my lucky day, because I recorded a class-A EVP! It was loud, as if it came over my shoulder that said, "Contessa." I didn't review the audio until we arrived home.

The next summer, we revisited the abandoned high school once again. We looked though the class photos hanging on the walls but did not find a

Contessa. We did see four ladies whose first initial began with a C. The class photos only showed first initials.

We also heard a disembodied voice we believe to had said, "Please help me with this." My wife heard words as if someone blared a radio and other strange noises.

Whoever these school spirits may be, they seem to be true to their school and have caused no harm to the visiting teams of ghost investigators.

10

YUMA COUNTY

The Mary Elizabeth Post Elementary School building is located at 400 Fifth Avenue in Yuma, Arizona, and is named in honor of Yuma's pioneer of education, Mary Elizabeth Post. She was respected as an educator who was involved with women in politics. In 1903, she organized the first women's club in Yuma. Mary worked tirelessly to establish the Carnegie Library in Yuma, where she served as a lifelong member of the board.

Post came to Yuma in 1872. A native of Elizabethtown, New York, Mary Elizabeth had a difficult time accepting the lawlessness of the Wild West in the Arizona Territory. History books say she sent her students home during hangings that were conducted next to her schoolhouse to keep the children from watching them.

Her father was a carpenter who loved literature and taught Post and her seven siblings the importance of education and manners in society. Anticipating a great future for his daughter, Post's father hired a teacher to educate her further during the summer. Post was an avid student and took on her first teaching job in 1856 at the young age of fifteen. Mary Elizabeth applied for a scholarship at the University of Vermont, not knowing that

Mary Elizabeth Post School. *Wikimedia.*

the university did not accept female students. Since Mary Elizabeth was a determined woman, this rejection did not going stop her from furthering her education. She went on to study at the Burlington Female Seminary. After graduating in 1863, Post relocated with her family to Iowa.

After settling in Iowa, Post fell in love with a politician who was a rising star in his party. While he was campaigning for an important political position, his political enemies, aware that he was about to win the election, began spreading spiteful rumors that he was having an affair. The rumors were just that—rumors! But Post felt betrayed and embarrassed. Mary Elizabeth was deeply hurt and avoided her love interest for the rest of her life—even refusing to speak to him or respond to his pleading letters. She soon accepted a teaching job in Lansing, Iowa. While in Lansing, Post began digging deeper into her former lover's supposed affair. Despite discovering the truth, she chose not to apologize to him.

Post moved to Arizona City, Arizona (now Yuma, Arizona), in 1872. She was greeted by Arizona territorial governor Anson P.K. Safford. Post was the fifth teacher in Arizona, and with the aid of Safford, she reopened a former saloon and converted it into Arizona's third school.

Post gained a reputation for being a strict rule enforcer in class. If a student dared to miss class, Post would tromp over to their home, and unless the student had a true and valid excuse to not be in class, she would haul them back to school herself! Many of her students' parents disliked her stern practices, and Post was well aware of this. In time, she began winning the parents over. She eventually ordered fashionable uniforms from San Francisco and taught the students' mothers how to sew.

On May 2, 1873, Mary witnessed the hanging of Manuel Fernandez, who had been found guilty of murdering Michael "Rawhide" McCartney, a local salesman. Disheartened by the act and with subsequent support from the editors of the *Arizona Sentinel*, Post decided to leave Arizona City and relocate to San Diego, California. There, she took on the job of general vice-principal for San Diego's school system. A year later, she returned to Arizona City. Mary Elizabeth and her brother Albert shared teaching positions at her new school; Mary supervised the girls while Albert oversaw the boys.

Like the teachers of today, Post did not hesitate to fundraise for education. Stories say she once convinced a wealthy gentleman to organize a charity horse race that raised $600, which she used to buy school supplies. This

was a large sum of money in those times! She even talked a Colorado River boat captain into organizing a beauty contest, from which she collected another $500, which was also used for school supplies.

After Post retired from teaching at the age of seventy-two in 1913, the United States Senate passed a bill that endowed her a pension of fifty dollars a month. In her retirement, Mary Elizabeth operated a small shop and pursued her hobby of sewing, going door to door teaching women and girls how to sew clothes. Mary Elizabeth Post died of natural causes in 1934. She was ninety-three years old. The Mary E. Post School was built in 1940 in Yuma.

It is believed Mary Elizabeth continues to watch over the community with a ruler firmly in hand. Former students of the Mary E. Post School have claimed they saw her ghost its haunted hallways. The building is now an auditorium with offices. A portrait of Post still hangs in the hallway of the school building,

Mary Elizabeth Post's portrait. *Find a Grave.*

and it has been said her eyes in the picture move back and forth, following people unexpectedly as they casually walk down the corridor.

Phoenix Channel 3/5 news reporter/cameraman Gibby Parra noted that while growing up in Yuma, he attended Mary E. Post School. If you were a disobedient student, you were required to walk down the hallway, past the spooky portrait, on your way to the principal's office. Some teachers offered a bargaining sentence—walk past the intimidating painting or take a paddling in class.

"Most of us boys would more than likely opt to take the paddling," Gibby nodded. "That picture was so creepy! It's true what they say; the eyes would follow you all the way down the hallway. We would look down at the ground, walk steadily—but peek out of the corner of our eye. You sort of took a deep breath and went for it! I will never forget that portrait—everyone's worst nightmare!"

11
TEACHER AND STUDENT RULES IN THE EARLY YEARS

The sources for these "rules" are unknown. This writer cannot prove their authenticity—only their legitimacy and charming quaintness. These lists have been printed up for years and have appeared independently on various websites and in newspapers. It is no wonder that many of our historic schools are haunted—enjoy!

1872 RULES FOR TEACHERS

1. Teachers, each day, will fill lamps and clean chimneys.
2. Each morning, teacher will bring a bucket of water and a scuttle of coal for the daily session.
3. Make your pens carefully. You may whittle nibs to the individual taste of the pupils.
4. Men teachers may take one evening each week for courting purposes, or two evenings a week if they attend church regularly.
5. After ten hours in school, the teachers may spend the remaining time reading the Bible or other good book.
6. Women teachers who marry or engage in unseemly conduct will be dismissed.

7. Every teacher should lay aside from each pay day a goodly sum of his earnings for his benefit during his declining years so that he will not become a burden on society.
8. Any teacher who smokes, uses liquor in any form, frequents pool or public halls or gets shaved in a barbershop will give good reason to suspect his worth, intention, integrity and honesty.
9. The teacher who performs his labor faithfully and without fault for five years will be given an increase of twenty-five cents per week in his pay, providing the board of education approves.
10. You may ride in a buggy with a man if the man is your father or your brother.

1872 STUDENT RULES

1. Respect your schoolmaster. Obey him and accept his punishments.
2. Do not call your classmates names or fight with them. Love and help each other.
3. Never make noise or disturb your neighbors as they work.
4. Be silent during class. Do not talk unless it is absolutely necessary.
5. Do not leave your seat without permission.
6. No more than one student at a time may go to the washroom.
7. At the end of class, wash your hands and face. Wash your feet if they are bare.
8. Bring firewood into the classroom for the stove whenever the teacher tells you to do this chore.
9. Go quietly in and out of the classroom.
10. If the schoolmaster calls your name after class, straighten the benches and tables. Sweep the room, dust and leave everything tidy.

1886 RULES FOR TEACHERS

1. Wash windows and clean classroom with soap and water once a week.
2. Check the outhouses daily.
3. Women are forbidden to wear a bathing costume in public at all times, bloomers for cycling, skirts slit to expose ankles or a bustle extension over ten inches.
4. Men may not wear a detachable collar or a necktie removed from shirt. Shirt sleeves cannot be unlinked and rolled. Hair must be closely cropped (unless bald or have disease of the scalp).
5. Cause for immediate dismissal includes frequenting the pool, marriage or other unseemly behavior by women teachers.
6. Joining of the feminist movement, such as the suffragettes, calls for dismissal.

VICTORIAN RULES FOR STUDENTS

1. Farmers and other persons possessing property are to pay for their children. When they write on paper—sixpence per week; when they write on slates—fourpence per week.
2. Children must attend school regularly.
3. Saturday is a whole holiday.
4. Hair must be neatly cut and combed.
5. Hands and face must be clean and clothes mended.
6. Girls, in particular, must be neat and without any finery.
7. If boys wear frocks on Sundays, they must be clean.
8. Every offence discovered against good order or good morals (disobedience of whatever kind, playing at games on the Sabbath, bad words, lying, cheating, stealing and mischief) will be strictly punished.

1915 RULES FOR TEACHERS

1. You will not marry during the term of your contract.
2. You are not to keep company with men.
3. You must be home between the hours of 8:00 p.m. and 6:00 a.m. unless attending a school function.
4. You may not loiter downtown in any of the ice cream stores.
5. You may not travel beyond the city limits unless you have permission of the chairman of the school board.
6. You may not smoke cigarettes.
7. You may not dress in bright colors.
8. You may, under no circumstances, dye your hair.
9. You must wear at least two petticoats.
10. Your dresses may not be any shorter than two inches above the ankles.
11. To keep the classroom neat and clean, you must sweep the floor once a day; scrub the floor with hot, soapy water once a week; clean the blackboards once a day; start the fire at 7:00 a.m. to have the school warm by 8:00 a.m., when the scholars arrive.

1923 RULES FOR TEACHERS

1. Not to get married. This contract becomes null and void immediately if the teacher marries.
2. Not to keep company with men.
3. To be at home between the hours of 8:00 p.m. and 6:00 a.m. unless in attendance at school function.
4. Not to loiter in downtown ice cream stores.
5. Not to leave town at any time without the permission of the chairman of the board of trustees.
6. Not to smoke cigarettes. This contract becomes null and void immediately if teacher is found smoking.
7. Not to drink beer, wine or whiskey. This contract becomes null and void immediately if teacher is found drinking beer, wine or whiskey.

8. Not to ride in an automobile with any man except her father or brother.
9. You cannot dress in bright colors or dye your hair.
10. You must keep the classroom clean.

1940 RULES FOR TEACHERS

1. Teachers became stricter with the students.
2. Teachers punished the students for bad behavior by either a spanking or by humiliation, which usually included wearing a dunce cap.
3. Teachers taught with a chalkboard and lectured while students took notes.
4. Teachers still taught in one-room schoolhouses.
5. Most teachers had rules, such as:
   a. Sit up straight at your desk with feet firmly on the floor.
   b. Stand up next to the desk when answering a question.
   c. Raise one finger to answer a question.
   d. Raise two fingers to use the bathroom.

1959 RULES FOR STUDENTS

1. Attend classes punctually and regularly.
2. Submit to such discipline as would be exercised by a kind, firm and judicious parent.
3. Be neat and clean in his person and habits, diligent in his studies, kind and courteous to his fellow students and obedient and respectful to the teachers.
4. Haircuts: These are to be of reasonable length, and no long sideburns. Hair should be neatly combed always. Girls are not to wear curlers of any kind.
5. Boots: Boots and shoes should be clean and polished. Heels with steal cleats are not allowed. Over shoes are not to be worn in the classroom.

6. Jackets: Boys may wear suit coats, sport jackets or cardigans. No black leather jackets are allowed in school.
7. No tight, low-waisted blue jeans will be allowed.
8. Skirts: Any type of skirt which is clean and pressed is acceptable for girls. The wearing of unwieldy crinoline skirts is discouraged.
9. Shirts and Blouses: Should be cleaned and pressed. They are to be worn with the collars turned down. Shirts should be long enough to be tucked inside of the waistband. Boys who wear V-necked sweaters must wear a shirt underneath.

1960 TEACHERS GUIDE

1. Teachers are to be in attendance at 8:50 a.m. Lessons cease at 3:50 p.m., but teachers may be required to be on duty until 4:00 p.m.
2. Teachers unable to attend should ring the office as soon as possible after 8:30 a.m. A medical certificate must be produced for absences of more than three consecutive days; otherwise, pay is deducted.
3. The bell is sounded to end a class period. A teacher should not delay a class or a pupil so that the next teacher's lesson is affected.
4. Teachers are not to allow students to go to their lockers in class time.
5. Girls are to be seated in the desks near the door. Teachers should remain in the classroom to supervise the dismissal of the class.
6. The blackboard must be left clean for the next class. Supplies are limited, and tests should be written on the blackboard whenever possible.
7. Teachers are requested to observe high standards of dress and behavior during school hours. This, of course, includes no smoking in classrooms.

Paranormal Resources: Teams and Tours

Arizona Desert Ghost Hunters: www.adghosthunters.com
Arizona Prism Paranormal: www.azprism.com
AZ Ghost Adventures: www.azghostadventures.com
AZ Paranormal: info@AZParanormal.com
Beelieve Paranormal: www.believeparanormal.com
Crossing Over Paranormal: www.thecopscrew.com
Friends of the Other Side: www.friendsoftheotherside.org
Ghost Patrol: www.facebook.com/Ghost-Patrol-
    136946729757887/?ref=page_internal
Ghost Town Tours, Jerome: www.ghosttowntours.org
Ladies Investigative Paranormal Society: LIPSParanormal@gmail.com
MVD Ghostchasers: www.mvdghostchasers.com
Phoenix, Arizona Paranormal Society: www.phoenix-arizona-paranormal-
    society.com
Phoenix Haunted History Tours: marshallshore@gmail.com
Southern Arizona Scientific Paranormal Investigators: www.SASPI.org
Verde Valley Spirit Seekers: www.facebook.com/groups/
    verdevalleyspiritseekers/about
Wicked City Ghost Tours: www.wickedcityghosttours.com

BIBLIOGRAPHY

Arizona Champion. "Fire at Emerson School." December 16, 1921.

————. "Miss Mabel Milligan a Beloved Local Teacher Died Suddenly Thursday." November 9, 1923.

Arizona Daily Sun. "Haunted Flagstaff—The Top 10 Spookiest Spots in Town." October 29, 2018.

Arizona News. "Ghost Cheerleaders! 4 Haunted High Schools in Arizona." August 14, 2018.

Arizona Republic. "Arizona State University." October 25, 2002.

————. "Compromise at Work in Patagonia." April 29, 2001.

————. "Devil's Advocates at ASU Share Campus Lore." August 17, 1990.

————. "Great, Small Pay Gammage Tribute." December 23, 1959.

Arizona Silver Belt. "Globe High School Year Book Staff Gathers Ghost Stories." August 2, 2023.

————. "Noftsger Hill Has Its Own Halloween Stories." October 22, 2003.

ASU Center for Creative Writing. "The Piper Writers House." April 19, 2021.

ASU News. "Tour ASU's 'Haunted' Hallowed Halls." October 27, 2021.

Berlin, Andi, and Samantha Munsey. "Take This Spooky Arizona Ghost Road Trip." *This Is Tucson*, June 21, 2021.

Branning, Debe. *Arizona's Haunted Route 66*. Charleston, SC: Arcadia Publishing, 2021.

————. *Dining with the Dead*. Phoenix, AZ: American Traveler Press, 2017.

————. *Grand Canyon Ghost Stories*. Malvern, PA: Riverbend Publishing, 2012.

————. *The Graveyard Shift*. Phoenix, AZ: American Traveler Press, 2012.

————. *Haunted Globe*. Charleston, SC: Arcadia Publishing, 2022.

————. *Haunted Phoenix*. Charleston, SC: Arcadia Publishing, 2019.

————. *Sleeping with Ghosts*. San Marino, CA: Golden West Publishers, 2004.

Bruner, Betsey. "NAU Ghost Stories." *Arizona Daily Sun*, October 30, 2001.

Channel 9 KGUN News Tucson. "Ruby Ariz. Is a Ghost Town with a Ghostly Past." September 5, 2022.

Channel 12 KPNX News Phoenix. 2023.

George Washington Carver Museum. www.gecmccaz.wordpress.com.

Gila County Historical Museum. "Globe High School History." January 10, 2019.

Glionna, John M. "Haunted High School Spooks Former Frontier Town." *Los Angeles Times*, May 25, 2013.

Golightly, Chase. "The Ghost in Gilbert High School and Other Weird Things Valley Police Officers Have Encountered." Haunted Places. www.hauntedplaces.org/state/arizona.

Jones, Cecil. "Gleeson UFO Leaves Traces." *Tucson Daily Citizen*, October 19, 1968.

Melbery, Virgil. "Death Unexpected for ASU President." *Arizona Republic*, December 23, 1959.

Nicholas, Samantha. "Old Tombstone High School Officially Sold After 15 Years." *Tombstone News*, May 6, 2022.

Pittnger, Angela. "Tombstone's Historic Union High School Property for Sale." *This Is Tucson*, August 19, 2014.

Powers, Francine. *Haunted Bisbee*. Charleston, SC: Arcadia Publishing, 2020.

————. *Haunted Cochise County*. Charleston, SC: Arcadia Publishing, 2023.

Sexton, Connie Cone, Annie Z. Yu and Kaila White. "Real Haunted Places in Metro Phoenix." October 5, 2015. AZCentral.com.

State Press. "Here Are the Spookiest Spots on and around ASU's Tempe Campus." November 1, 2018.

Street, Jessica. "The Haunted Chandler High School in Chandler AZ." *All Haunted Places*, October 23, 2022.

Tours of Jerome. www.toursofjerome.com.

Tucson Citizen. "Custodians Say There May Be a Ghost in Catalina High Halls." October 31, 1980.

UA News. "Fright On: Meet the Ghosts of the UA." October 29, 2014.

"What's in a Name." *Southwest Living in Yuma, Arizona*, October 5, 2018.

White, Kaila. "5 Haunted Places in the West Valley." October 30, 2014. AZCentral.com.

Wiley, Rick. "UFO's Hover Over Gleeson." *Arizona Daily Star*, November 30, 2017.

ABOUT THE AUTHOR

Debe Branning has been the director of the MVD Ghostchasers, a Mesa/Bisbee, Arizona–based paranormal team, since 1994. The team conducts investigations of haunted, historical locations throughout Arizona and has offered paranormal workshop/investigations since 2002. Debe has been a guest lecturer and speaker at several Arizona universities and community colleges, science fiction and paranormal conferences, historical societies and libraries.

Her television appearances include an episode of *Streets of Fear* for FearNet.com (2009), an episode of Travel Channel's *Ghost Stories* about haunted Jerome, Arizona (2010), and an episode of *Ghost Adventures*, "Old Gila County Jail and Courthouse" (2018). As a paranormal journalist, she has investigated haunted locations, including castles, jails, ships, inns and cemeteries, and has taken walking ghost tours in the United States, England, Scotland, Ireland and Mexico. She has been the guest of the Historic Hotels of the Rockies and U.S. tourism departments in Carlsbad, Salem and Biloxi.

Debe is the author of *Sleeping with Ghosts: A Ghost Hunter's Guide to AZ's Haunted Hotels and Inns* (2004), *Grand Canyon Ghost Stories* (2012), *The Graveyard Shift: Arizona's Historic and Haunted Cemeteries* (2012), *Dining with the Dead: Arizona's Historic and Haunted Restaurants and Cafés* (2017), *Haunted Phoenix* (2019), *Ghosts of Houston's Market Square Park* (2020), *Arizona's Haunted Route 66* (2021) and a series of three children's books, *The Adventures of Chickolet Pigolet: The Bribe of Frankenbeans*, *Murmur on the Oink Express* and *You Ought to be in Pig-tures*.

ABOUT THE MVD GHOSTCHASERS

Referenced frequently in this book, the group MVD Ghostchasers is one of the original three paranormal teams in Arizona still in operation under the same director since 1994. The team is based in Mesa, Arizona, and a second investigation team, added in 2007, is based in Bisbee, Arizona. In the group's early days, many of its members were either employees or past employees of the State of Arizona Motor Vehicle Division (MVD). In recent years, the group has expanded its membership to include valued investigators from all walks of life. Ghost hunting has become second nature to all of them. Paranormal investigations are approached professionally and performed with integrity. The team members are experts in the technical skills necessary to be in the paranormal field today. Through continued research and education, the MVD Ghostchasers have earned trust and respect from their clients and other paranormal investigators. They follow strict paranormal protocol guidelines that have made their group one of the most credible and valued teams in Arizona and the United States. Several members of the team are historians, authors and lecturers and have appeared on various reputable paranormal network programs. The leader and founder of the crew, Debe Branning, has organized investigations throughout Arizona and has arranged haunted road trips around the country. The team offers paranormal workshops for interested experienced paranormal investigators as well as beginning ghost hunters. This keeps the team busy the year-round. They have been the subjects of several newspaper articles that chronicle their ghostly activities, and they have been featured in magazines such as *Arizona Highway* magazine and AAA's *Highroad* magazine. MVD Ghostchasers have appeared on many internet programs as well as several local TV newscasts about Arizona hauntings. The group has formed a favorite yearly speaking panel at various statewide paranormal comicons. Team members have appeared on Fearnet.com's *Streets of Fear*, Syfy's *Ghost Hunters* and Travel Channel's *Ghost Stories*, *Deadly Possessions* and *Ghost Adventures*. The team partners with several paranormal investigation teams in Arizona and other parts of the United States.

FREE eBOOK OFFER

Scan the QR code below, enter your e-mail address and get our original Haunted America compilation eBook delivered straight to your inbox for free.

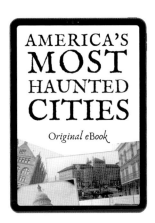

ABOUT THE BOOK

Every city, town, parish, community and school has their own paranormal history. Whether they are spirits caught in the Bardo, ancestors checking on their descendants, restless souls sending a message or simply spectral troublemakers, ghosts have been part of the human tradition from the beginning of time.

In this book, we feature a collection of stories from five of America's most haunted cities: Baltimore, Chicago, Galveston, New Orleans and Washington, D.C.

SCAN TO GET
AMERICA'S MOST HAUNTED CITIES

Having trouble scanning? Go to:
biz.arcadiapublishing.com/americas-most-haunted-cities

Visit us at
www.historypress.com